SWING TRADING

A Beginner's Guide to Investing in The Stock
Market, Including Most Profitable Strategies
and Trading Tools.

LUCAS BUNN

DISCLAIMER

All Erudition contained in this book is given for informational and educational purposes only. The author is not in any way accountable for any results or outcomes that emanate from using this material. Constructive attempts have been made to provide information that is both accurate and effective, but the author is not bound for accuracy or use/misuse of information.

FOREWORD

First, I will like to thank you for taking the first step of trusting me and deciding to purchase/read this life transforming eBook. Thanks for spending your time and resources on this material. I can assure you of exact blueprint I lay bare in the information manual you are currently reading. It has transformed lives, and I strongly believe it will equally transform your life too. All the information I presented in this Do-It-Yourself is easy to digest and practice.

TABLE OF CONTENTS

INTRODUCTION: WHAT IS
SWING TRADING?

The term alludes to the different styles of swing trading stock, index or commodities. This trading is a sort of trading practice where the trader purchases or sells the instrument at or extremely close to the finish of a down or up price swing in the commodity. This swing is caused either because of day by day price volatility or week by week price volatility. Information on these styles causes him become a gainful trader and places him on the way of fruitful trading profession.

The time limit that is normally associated with holding the instrument by the trader is 1-4 days. It is for the most part not exactly seven days regardless. The cash or the swing trading stock which the trader is managing in swings starting with one price level then onto the next. A swing trader rides on this swaying or swing that the market makes on the stock. That implies he purchases the instruments in the direction of market trends and he doesn't trade by conflicting with the significant trends in the market.

There are various manners by which he can put a trade. The most well-known method for doing it in the direction of market trend is to sit tight at the costs swing trading stock to return or backtrack and afterward enter a trade before it goes onwards. This is the most secure strategy as he can stack the chances in support of him by watching the higher timeframe charts and afterward enters the trade in the direction of significant trend likewise got back to the force time. There are some essential components of swing trading that should be aced to turn into a fruitful trader.

The as a matter of first importance element in learning the swing trading business is a comprehension of the trading psychology. The other significant angle requires a knowledge into the significant trends of the market. This encourages him to recognize accurately the trend in the market and addition from it. The third significant viewpoint is obviously the trader's capacity to oversee cash with the goal that he can expand gains and limit dangers. The trader ought to likewise have the option to peruse and comprehend the Japanese Candlestick formation so as to get a vibe of the market sentiments. Another element that is urgent to his prosperity is to have the option to discover the best trading hours to open and close the trade.

Different fundamentals of a decent trader are to find what indicators are utilized by other professional traders to run swing trading effectively. He should likewise be knowledgeable with the Trading indicators utilized by different banks. He ought to likewise possess the option to recognize the specialized market analysis and the major market analysis as two most significant styles to break down the market. Among other element of the swing trading business is the information on help and resistance levels, Fibonacci retracement level, stop misfortune and recognizable proof of trend lines.

The way toward swing exchanging has turned into a well-known stock exchanging technique utilized by numerous dealers over the market. This style of exchanging has demonstrated to be exceptionally effective for some dedicated stocks and Forex dealers. Customarily swing exchanging has been characterized as a progressively theoretical methodology as the positions are generally purchased and held for the dealers foreordained time allotment. These time allotments could run somewhere in the range of two days to a couple of months. The objective of the swing broker is to distinguish the pattern either up or down and place their exchanges the most invaluable position. From that point the merchant will ride the pattern to what they decide as the depletion point and sell for a benefit. Intermittently swing brokers will use a wide range of specialized markers that will enable them to have a progressively worthwhile likelihood when making their exchanges. Shorter-term brokers don't really will in general swing exchange as they lean toward holding positions for the duration of the day and practicing them preceding the end of the market. Swing exchanging technique uses time and it is this time is the impediment factor for a long time dealers. Generally there is a lot of hazard associated with the end of the market and that a merchant won't acknowledge this hazard.

Swing exchanging is a style of exchanging that endeavors to catch increases a stock (or any monetary instrument) over a time of a couple of days to a little while. Swing brokers principally utilize specialized investigation to search for exchanging openings. These brokers may use principal examination notwithstanding breaking down value patterns and examples

Swing exchanging is a more extended term exchanging style that expects persistence to hold your exchanges for a few days one after another. It is perfect for the individuals who can't screen their outlines for the duration of the day however can devote two or three hours examining the market each night.

This is likely most appropriate for the individuals who have all day employments or school yet have enough extra time to keep awake to-date with what is happening in the worldwide economies.

Swing exchanging endeavors to recognize "swings" inside a medium-term pattern and enter just when there is by all accounts a high likelihood of winning.

For instance, in an upturn, you intend to purchase (go long) at "swing lows." And on the other hand, sell (go short) at "swing highs" to exploit transitory countertrends.

Since exchanges last any longer than one day, bigger stop misfortunes are required to climate instability, and a forex merchant must adjust that to their cash the board plan.

You will in all likelihood observe exchanges conflict with you during the holding time since there can be numerous variances of the value during the shorter time spans.

It is significant that you can try to avoid panicking during these occasions and trust in your examination.

Since exchanges more often than not have bigger targets, spreads won't have as quite a bit of an effect on your general benefits.

Thus, exchanging sets with bigger spreads and lower liquidity is worthy.

You should be a swing dealer if:

You wouldn't fret holding your exchanges for a few days.

You are eager to take less exchanges however progressively cautious to ensure your exchanges are generally excellent arrangements.

You wouldn't fret having enormous stop misfortunes.

You are understanding.

You can resist the urge to panic when exchanges move against you.

You might NOT have any desire to be a swing dealer if:

You like quick paced, activity stuffed exchanging.

You are fretful and like to know whether you are correct or wrong right away.

You get sweat-soaked and on edge when exchanges conflict with you.

You can't put in two or three hours consistently to break down the business sectors.

You can't surrender your World of Warcraft striking sessions.

The differentiation of swing exchanging is an expansive point in that it has various impacts from a huge number of various exchanging procedures. These exchanging procedures are interesting and have their particular hazard profiles. Swing exchanging can be a great path for a market member to further improve their specialized investigation abilities while allowing them a chance to give more consideration to the principal side of exchanging. Numerous fruitful swing brokers have been known to utilize a bollinger band procedure as an apparatus to help them in entering and leaving positions. Obviously, for a swing dealer to be fruitful at the methodology, they should have a high bent for deciding the present market pattern and putting their situations as per that pattern. It does a swing dealer note great to put a short position with the arrangement of holding for an all-inclusive timeframe in a market that is plainly slanting upwards. The general subject here is that the objective of the dealers ought to be to build their likelihood of progress while restricting or wiping out hazard totally. The swing dealer's most noticeably awful foe is that of a sideways or in dynamic market. Sideways value activity will stop a swing merchant cold in their tracks as there is no overall pattern to key off of.

At the point when utilized effectively swing exchanging is a superb system utilized by numerous merchants crosswise over different various markets. It isn't just utilized in the Forex showcase however it is a key apparatus in fates and value markets. Swing dealers take the abilities that they learn through specialized examination and can even parlay these aptitudes into different alternatives techniques. The transient idea of swing exchanging separates it from that of the conventional speculator. Speculators will in general have a more extended term time skyline and are not customarily influenced by momentary value variances. As usual, one must recollect that swing exchanging is just a single technique and ought to be used just when properly comprehended. Like any exchanging systems swing exchanging can be unsafe and preservationist methodologies can transform into day exchanging procedures rapidly. If you intend to utilize a swing exchanging system, guarantee that you completely comprehend the dangers and build up a technique that will have the option to enable you to produce greatest rate returns on your positions.

Swing exchanging is one of exchanging styles which generally executed in theoretical action in monetary markets, for example, securities, item, remote trade, stock and stock record. Normally this exchanging style requires a swing dealer to hold their exchanging position more than one exchanging day, generally 2 to 5 exchanging days. Swing exchanging is mainstream in exchanging world as this exchanging styles for the most part has a decent hazard and reward proportion, it implies the likelihood to pick up benefit is greater than the hazard that may ascend in each exchange.

By and large, swing exchanging goes for 100 pips benefit likelihood. Benefit potential can be picked up from each market swing. A swing broker, particularly in remote trade and stock file advertise, can go both long or short to accept each open door. It likewise implies, inside an exchanging week, when a market is unpredictable, a swing dealer may run over a few exchanging openings the individual in question can take.

Contrasted with scalping exchanging or day exchanging, clearly swing exchanging has less exchanging chances, notwithstanding, as should be obvious here If you execute this exchanging style, most likely you will have more opportunity to do your different exercises as you don't need to keep your eyes on a market all the exchanging day. Obviously you will just get less chances however with high likelihood to win for every chance. It is your call to pick which exchanging style to apply. No exchanging style is immaculate, there is constantly in addition to and short.

Presently, If you surely need to give an attempt to swing exchanging, you can discover a few procedures from numerous assets accessible in the web. You may discover a few books and some other instructive materials on swing exchanging. You can visit and be an individual from some exchanging discussions too. Notwithstanding, as regular I need to advise you that there are likewise some shifty individuals guaranteeing themselves as swing exchanging masters however they simply need you to purchase their refuse training materials. Simply be mindful so as to such individuals.

Luckily, in the wake of getting some essential comprehension and experience on swing exchanging, you can be a decent swing merchant also. You can even think of your own swing exchanging systems. Numerous individuals appreciate the advantage of building up their own swing exchanging systems as they are the main ones who realize their exchanging character, need and style. Never quit to figure out how to be a decent swing merchant, in spite of the fact that unquestionably it will require some investment to ace swing exchanging brilliantly yet at last the majority of your endeavors will pay out.

Issues With Swing Trading Using Options

Swing exchanging is one of the most widely recognized methods for exchanging the securities exchange.

Regardless of whether you know it or not, you presumably have been swing exchanging all these while. Swing exchanging is purchasing every so often selling a couple of days or weeks after the fact when costs are higher, or lower (on account of a short). Such a cost increment or lessening is known as a "Value Swing", subsequently the expression "Swing Trading".

Most learners to choices exchanging take up choices as a type of influence for their swing exchanging. They need to purchase call choices when costs are low and afterward rapidly sell them a couple of days or weeks after the fact for an utilized addition. The other way around valid for put choices. In any case, numerous such amateurs immediately discovered the most difficult way possible that in choices swing exchanging, they could in any case make a generous misfortune regardless of whether the stock inevitably moved toward the path that they anticipated.

How is that so? What are a few issues related with swing exchanging utilizing alternatives that they neglected to observe?

For sure, despite the fact that choices can be utilized just as utilized substitution for exchanging the basic stock, there are a couple of things about alternatives that most tenderfoots neglect to observe.

1) Strike Price

It doesn't take long for anybody to understand that there are numerous alternatives accessible crosswise over many strike costs for every single optionable stock. The undeniable decision that fledglings generally make is to purchase the "modest" out of the cash alternatives for higher influence. Out of the cash choices are alternatives that have no worked in an incentive in them. These are call alternatives with strike costs higher than the overarching stock cost or put choices with strike costs lower than the overall stock cost.

The issue with purchasing out of the cash alternatives in swing exchanging is that regardless of whether the basic stock move toward your expectation (upwards for purchasing call choices and downwards for purchasing put choices), you could at present lose ALL your cash if the stock didn't surpass the strike cost of the choices you purchased! The truth is out, this is known as to "Lapse Out Of The Money" which makes every one of the choices you purchased useless. This is likewise how most fledglings lose all their cash in choices exchanging.

By and large, the more out of the cash the choices are, the higher the influence and the higher the hazard that those alternatives will terminate useless, losing all of you the cash put into them. The more in the cash the choices are, the lower increasingly costly they are because of the worth incorporated with them, the lower the influence turns out to be nevertheless the lower the danger of terminating useless. You have to take the normal extent of the move and the measure of hazard you can mull over when choosing which strike cost to purchase for swing exchanging with choices. If you anticipate a major move, out of the cash choices would obviously give you gigantic rewards yet If the move neglects to surpass the strike cost of those choices by termination, a terrible arousing is standing by.

2) Expiration Date

Not at all like swing exchanging with stocks which you can clutch never-endingly when things turn out badly, alternatives have a distinct lapse date. This implies If you are incorrect, you will rapidly lose cash when lapse lands without the advantage of having the option to clutch the position and hang tight for an arrival or profit.

Indeed, swing exchanging with choices is battling against time. The quicker the stock moves, the more sure you are of benefit. Uplifting news is, all optionable stocks have choices crosswise over numerous termination months too. Closer month choices are less expensive and further month alternatives are progressively costly. All things considered, If you are sure that the hidden stock is going to move rapidly, you could exchange with closer termination month alternatives or what we call "Front Month Options", which are less expensive and subsequently have a higher influence.

Real World Example of Swing Trade in Apple

The diagram above demonstrates a period where Apple (AAPL) had a solid value move higher. This was trailed by a little cup and handle design which frequently flag a continuation of the value rise if the stock moves over the high of the handle.

For this situation, the cost rises over the handle, setting off a conceivable purchase close $192.70.

One conceivable spot to put a stop misfortune is beneath the handle, set apart by the square shape, close $187.50.

In view of the section and stop misfortune, the evaluated hazard for the exchange is $5.20 per share ($192.70 - $187.50).

If searching for a potential reward that is in any event double the hazard, any cost above $203.10 ($192.70 +(2 *$5.20)) will give this.

Beside a hazard/remunerate, the merchant could likewise use other leave techniques, for example, trusting that the cost will make an extraordinary failure. With this strategy, a leave sign wasn't given until $216.46, when the value dipped under the earlier pullback low. This strategy would have brought about a benefit of $23.76 per share. Thought of another way: a 12% benefit in return for under 3% chance. This swing exchange took roughly two months.

Other leave strategies could be the point at which the value crosses beneath a moving normal (not appeared), or when a pointer, for example, the stochastic oscillator crosses its sign line.

Exchange forex and CFDs on stock files, products, stocks, metals and energies with an authorized and controlled representative. For all customers who open their first genuine record, XM offers up to $5000 store reward to test the XM items and administrations with no underlying store required. Study how you can exchange more than 1000 instruments on the XM MT4 and MT5 stages from your PC and Mac, or from an assortment of cell phones.

The amount Money Do I Need to Swing Trade Stocks?

Keen on swing exchanging stocks–taking exchanges that last a couple of days to half a month and thinking about what amount of cash you have to begin? How much capital you'll need is reliant on the procedure you use, which at that point influences the amount you chance per exchange and your position size. This article gives different situations to how a lot of money you'll have to swing exchange stocks a hazard controlled way, which will improve your opportunity of accomplishment.

Markets You Can Swing Trade

Swing exchanging is taking a place that could most recent daily to half a month (possibly several months for certain brokers/exchanges). To what extent a swing exchange keeps going relies upon the procedure you're utilizing and what you anticipate from your exchanges.

If a stock normally moves 1% every day, and it needs to move 10% so as to arrive at your objective (where you need to get out with a benefit), it could take half a month or more before the value advances toward your leave point (if current conditions proceed).

Swing brokers hold positions medium-term, in contrast to informal investors (perceive How Much Money Do I Require to Become a Day Trader?) who close all situations before the day closes. Procedures shift by swing dealer, however the primary spotlight is on force swing merchants need to catch a conventional piece of value development in the most limited measure of time conceivable. At the point when the value energy closes, swing brokers proceed onward to different chances.

This style of exchanging should be possible in many markets (stocks, forex, fates and choices, for instance) which have development you can benefit from (profit!). Swing exchanging stocks is well known on the grounds that there's constantly a stock moving with force some place

Forex is likewise mainstream in light of the fact that for the most part there's a money pair (or a few) that is moving admirably. Prospects are likewise exceptionally mainstream among day and swing merchants, offering a wide cluster of items, (for example, gold, bonds, stock records, instability, espresso, and so forth) to exchange. Swing exchanging forex requires less capital than stocks and fates, and is hence a decent choice If you need more cash-flow to swing exchange stocks.

How about we take a look at certain situations in the financial exchange, so you can perceive how a lot of cash you'll have to turn into a securities exchange swing merchant.

Issue of Under-Capitalization When Swing Trading Stocks

Having more capital in your record is superior to less. One major slip-up dealers make is being under-promoted. In the stock, advertise being under-promoted can without much of a stretch occur... particularly to new brokers if their record drops in worth.

As showed, to make it worth our time and energy we ought to chance in any event $100 per exchange. Along these lines our victors won't be fundamentally disintegrated by commissions and expenses. However, If we hazard $100, what occurs if a dealer's record parity drops to $4,000? Presently they are gambling 2.5% on each exchange. If things still do not go smoothly, and the parity drops to $3,000, the broker is currently gambling 3.3% per exchange... they are gambling more as their presentation deteriorates!

If your record parity dips under $5,000, STOP TRADING, since you can never again bear to lose $100 and still keep the record hazard to under 2%. Likewise, If you opened a record with $15,000 and you said you would just hazard 1% exchange, if your parity falls beneath $10,000, quit exchanging. If you continue exchanging with an equalization beneath $10,000 you will hazard over 1% (gambling at any rate $100 per exchange).

Top up your record to bring it back above $5,000 (or $10,000 if gambling 1%) If you are as yet certain about your technique (or are eager to place in an opportunity to make it work), or just pick not to exchange until you are in a superior situation to do as such.

Cash Needed to Swing Trade Stocks – Final Word

The snappiest method to perceive how a lot of capital you need is to utilize the pursued equation:

exchange chance x position size x (100%/account hazard %) = Capital Required.

Expect you chance 1% of your record, purchase 100 offers and your exchange hazard is $2 (purchase at $38 and stop misfortune at $36). Module the numbers:

$2 x 100 x 100 = $20,000. That is the amount you have to make that exchange. You could use influence (up to 2:1) which implies that you really need $10K in the record to make this exchange, in light of the fact that with influence you will have the required $20K. Obviously you will need to have more in the record than the definite sum you need!

In case you're willing to chance 2% of your record per exchange:

$2 x 100 x 50 = $10,000 capital needed.

Record hazard and exchange hazard help you decide how much capital you will require. Each exchange is somewhat unique, with various exchange dangers and position sizes. Record for that when deciding the amount you will store. Concentrate the stock graphs, choose how and where you will enter and where you will put a stop misfortune.

When in doubt you will require at any rate $5,000 to $10,000 to swing exchange stocks successfully. It is prescribed you store more than the base, supposing that you store the absolute minimum a couple losing exchanges will put you beneath the suggest record balance.

It's smarter to hold up a couple of months and set aside more capital than to surge in under-promoted and likely lose everything. Utilize an opportunity to rehearse while you set aside!

What Swing Trading Is to You:

Deciding Your Time Commitment

Beginning in swing trading requires some reflection. Before you rush out to buy that smooth PC or set up your brokerage account, you have to consider what kind of swing trader you need to be. (Truly, swing traders come in various shapes and sizes.)

Your initial step is to determine exactly how much time you can focus on swing trading. You might be a full-time trader for a firm, in which case you ought to think about yourself as trading for a living. Or on the other hand you might be doing this part time for income with the expectation (and any desire for) turning into a full-time trader.

A plethora of swing traders have full-time jobs and have brief period to devote to trading, so they trade fundamentally to improve the returns of their venture accounts. Or then again maybe they're as of now in retirement and swing trade to develop their assets after some time. These swing traders monitors the market during the day yet depend on orders set outside market hours to enter or leave their positions. What's more, if they trade in charge conceded accounts, similar to an Individual Retirement Account, they can overlook the expense issue.

The fact of the matter is, you can swing trade whether you make some full-memories job or not, however you have to make alterations relying upon whether you're ready to watch the market throughout the day. What's more, incidentally, watching the market throughout the day doesn't really improve your returns. Truth be told, doing so can bring down them if it makes you overtrade or respond to market gyrations.

Swing trading as your essential source of income

If you expect to swing trade as your essential methods for producing income, be set up to go through a while — if not years — picking up understanding before you're ready to surrender your job and trade from home full time. Swing traders who trade full time devote a few hours per day to trading. They inquire about potential trades previously, during, and reseller's exchange hours. What's more, they handle pressure well.

Numerous traders find that they can't deal with the pressure of trading full time. All things considered, if swing trading is your fundamental wellspring of income, you face a great deal of strain to produce steady profits. What's more, you might be more enticed to gamble in the event that you experience a series of misfortunes. What numerous traders neglect to acknowledge is that the right reaction to a progression of misfortunes isn't all the more trading yet less trading. Make a stride back and assess the circumstance.

Swing trading for a living isn't troublesome as in to exceed expectations at it requires some kind of astounding IQ level or crazy work ethic. Or maybe, it requires a mind boggling measure of patience, discipline, and quiet. A swing trader who trades for income should consistently be dispassionate. At the point when things don't work out, the individual in question doesn't attempt to settle the score however proceeds onward to another chance.

So don't stop your day job since you produce amazing profits for a couple of months. The name of this game is to consistently have enough capital to return and play once more. If you plan on living off of $5,000 every month, for instance, you can't hope to produce that kind of profit on $30,000 of capital. That would require a month to month increase of 16.67 percent! The absolute best untouched traders on the planet beat out at returns of 20 to 25 percent every year more than 20 or 30 years.

Swing trading to enhance income or improve business returns

This class likely applies to the a lot of swing traders. Swing trading with an eye on winning extra income or improving the returns on your portfolio is less distressing than swing trading for a living. Despite everything you make them thing to depend on in the event that you commit an error, and you can swing trade while holding down a full-time job.

Part-time swing traders frequently do their examination when they return home from work and afterward execute trades the next day. Despite the fact that they will be unable to watch the market constantly, they can enter stop misfortune requests to protect their capital.

If you need to in the end swing trade full time, you ought to experience this stage first. After some time, you'll have the option to determine how well you've done. Also, if you follow different proposals in this book (like keeping a trading diary, which I spread in Chapter 3), you'll gain from your missteps and improve your systems.

Swing trading part time is reasonable for those people who

- Make some full-memories job

- Can devote a couple of hours seven days to breaking down markets and securities
- Have an enthusiasm for monetary markets and momentary trading
- Have the discipline to reliably put in stop misfortune requests
- Are accomplishing disappointing returns in their present venture portfolios from a monetary guide or outsider
- Don't gamble with their very own money and are probably not going to fall prey to multiplying down or facing significant challenges

In the event that you fit these criteria, at that point part-time swing trading might be for you. At the point when you first begin, I prescribe swing trading with only a little bit of your portfolio so any early slip-ups don't prove excessively exorbitant. In spite of the fact that paper trading can be valuable, it can't come close to the feelings you'll fight as a swing trader when you put your own money at stake.

Swing trading for no particular reason

Some swing traders get a rush from buying and selling securities in which they sometimes profit and sometimes lose. Their inspiration isn't to give or enhance current income. Or maybe, these swing traders do it for the excitement that originates from watching positions they buy and sell go here and there. Obviously, this can prompt huge misfortunes in the event that they abandon the principles intended to protect their capital — decides that I plot all through this book (explicitly in Chapter 10).

If you need to swing trade exclusively for fun, my recommendation is: don't. I suggest that you get your kicks at a bowling alley or b-ball court. The threat of trading for fun is that you're utilizing genuine money with genuine results. You may start to hazard a greater amount of your capital to fulfill your requirement for excitement. If you lose, you may make extraordinary move to prove yourself directly at last, such as placing all your money into a couple of securities. By then you're truly in the domain of betting.

If you demand trading for fun, at any rate confine yourself to a modest quantity of your assets and never contact your retirement savings. Recollect that you're contending with traders who are roused by profit, not simply excitement. That gives them a preferred position over somebody who just appreciates the game.

Swing Trading - How to Trade?

Fundamental learning:

It sounds incredible when you consider swing stock exchanging, however the majority of the brokers are unconscious of the technique on the best way to exchange. In swing exchanging the merchant by and large revels into buying the stocks toward the path where the pattern is solid. In straightforward words, the swing merchant will never exchange the course which isn't in the stream and not coordinating up the pattern. These exchanges are hung on for couple of days and as a rule they monitor the higher time allotment outlines which is around 1 hour and more than that while you are observing and setting your exchanges.

There are a few recognized manners by which a swing dealer can without much of a stretch spot his/her exchanges and that additionally toward the prevalent pattern. The normal and helpful practice is to sit tight at the cost level to remake previously and you have to enter your exchange before it reaches out towards on stream. The passage is done for the most part based on value resounding off of help or opposition levels, pattern lines or by and large it might require marker check.

In swing stock exchanging, the swing financial specialists or brokers can without much of a stretch have the chances heaped in their benefit by watching the more prominent and greater time span graphs and by entering the exchanges just the method for significant patterns in the securities exchange. Along these lines it will make your business an incredible style of exchanging regardless of the securities exchange.

Figure out How to Swing Trade: In request to figure out how to swing exchange, you have to have the authority over the central segments of the exchanging. Every one of the subtleties that are talked about underneath structures the structure hinders for the swing stock exchanging and are the reasons why outrageous expert financial specialists are extremely beneficial.

This territory grasps the accompanying:

o Trading brain science -

You have to create adjusted Psychology so as to wind up fit for exchanging effectively.

o Money the executives -

This administration allows a merchant to limit the dangers and to expand the arrival esteem on their rewards.

o Market investigation -

So as to do the market assessment, there are two different ways that are Technical and essential investigation.

o Japanese candle graphs -

It is the main component to have an inside investigate the financial exchange and its feelings. You should be equipped for perusing and understanding the Japanese candle arrangements.

o Trend Identification -

The swing brokers increment their chances by exchanging the course of the pattern. You have to discover the right pattern.

o Support and opposition levels -

These two levels grant the merchant to locate the pivotal degrees of the securities exchange where the patterns are in the dealer's support.

o Fibonacci retracement levels -

Much the same as the help and obstruction levels the Fibonacci retracement levels additionally enable you to have a decent passage in to the market.

o Trading markers -

The apprentices must take a gander at the pointers which are commonly utilized by the banks and expert financial specialists in swing exchanging.

o Stop misfortune -

Stop misfortunes bring about only a little harm; accordingly, it is disregarded by the majority of the newcomers around here.

o Trading hours -

Continuously cause a decent search and after that to find your own hours that are appropriate for the opening and shutting of the trades.......

Swing Trading: Swing Trading Stock That Help You Earn More

The term alludes to the different styles of swing exchanging stock, items or list. This exchanging is a sort of exchanging practice where the merchant purchases or sells the instrument at or close to the finish of a down or up value swing in the ware. This swing is caused either because of day by day value unpredictability or week by week value instability. Information of these styles encourages him become a beneficial dealer and puts him on the way of effective exchanging calling.

The time furthest reaches that is typically associated with holding the instrument by the merchant is 1-4 days. It is for the most part not exactly seven days regardless. The money or the swing exchanging stock which the merchant is managing in swings starting with one value level then onto the next. A swing broker rides on this wavering or swing that the market makes on the stock. That implies he purchases the instruments toward market patterns and he doesn't exchange by conflicting with the significant patterns in the market.

There are various manners by which he can put an exchange. The most well-known method for doing it toward market pattern is to sit tight at the costs swing exchanging stock to return or backtrack and afterward enter an exchange before it goes onwards. This is the most secure technique as he can stack the chances in support of him by watching the higher time span graphs and after that enters the exchange the bearing of significant pattern likewise got back to the draw time. There are some essential components of swing exchanging that should be aced to turn into an effective dealer.

The above all else component in learning the swing exchanging business is a comprehension of the exchanging brain research. The other significant viewpoint requires a knowledge into the significant patterns of the market. This causes him to distinguish effectively the pattern in the market and increase from it. The third significant viewpoint is obviously the dealer's capacity to oversee cash with the goal that he can expand gains and limit dangers. The dealer ought to likewise have the option to peruse and comprehend the Japanese Candlestick development so as to get a vibe of the market opinions. Another component that is urgent to his prosperity is to have the option to discover the best exchanging hours to open and close the exchange.

Different fundamentals of a decent merchant are to find what pointers are utilized by other expert dealers to run swing exchanging effectively. He should likewise be knowledgeable with the Trading markers utilized by different banks. He ought to likewise have the option to distinguish the specialized market investigation and the essential market examination as two most significant styles to break down the market. Among other component of the swing exchanging business is the information of help and obstruction levels, Fibonacci retracement level, stop misfortune and recognizable proof of pattern lines.

The dealer needs to acclimate himself with this data so as to begin his voyage to turning into an effective swing broker.

Swing Trading Stocks - An Insight to Pros and Cons

There are sure contrasts between Swing Trading Stocks and Day Trading. Day Trading is identified with a specific timeframe, though Swing exchanging likewise delineates a specific timeframe. Swing exchanging includes a timespan that is longer than the staring off into space time range and shorter than somebody who is headed to contribute and exchange for a more extended timeframe. If there should be an occurrence of records and assessment purposes, whatever is not exactly a year is imagined as a transient exchanging the financial exchange and anything that is about multi year or more is considered as long haul evaluating.

Swing exchanging is a novel style of exchanging and venture. It is reasonable for each one of the individuals who need to exchange for a more extended timeframe than a day exchanging and have a decent learning of swing exchanging procedures. The informal investors enter and exit around the same time and at a similar position. The swing merchants would leave their exchange of stocks and items to be open for couple of weeks which can stretch out as long as couple of months. The merchants work as indicated by the swing exchanging methodologies they know.

Swing Trading Stocks Pros and Cons:

Like all other things,Swing exchanging additionally has its great side and awful side. Bothe the day exchanging and swing exchanging are similarly dangerous which relies upon the experience, specialized assessment and brain science as upheld by the merchant. Continuously recollect the standard that is the more drawn out the time of exchange the market the higher the hazard factor.

The Pros of Swing Trading Stocks-

*It is less tedious than the day exchanging segment.

*A dealer possesses more energy for the assessment of the best exchanging methods between the exchanges and thusly, the broker can most likely choose great and fascinating entertainers.

*The first section which is poor is offered time to get recuperated from the harm and afterward go to a positive level or state contingent upon the bearing the merchant has chosen. It is prescribed that long position that is upward positions are substantially more superior to the principal short position that is descending position.

*Swing Traders doesn't require to address the issues of the 'Example Day Trader'.

*Swing merchants are permitted to have more information for concentrate as indicated by the time span than the informal investors.

*A swing broker is progressively sure and certain about his/her exchange in light of the fact that the ongoing pattern of exchanging is bolstered by the long haul information from the history.

The Cons of Swing Trading Stocks-

*Definitely the swing trader consumes less time and possesses more energy for the assessment of the best exchanging methods between the exchanges and accordingly, the dealer can likely choose great and fascinating entertainers.

The con: is that a swing merchant may get awful information and subtleties into the information assessment and might choose a less valuable stock execution or lost stock or item.

*The first passage which is poor is offered time to get recuperated from the harm and after that go to a positive level or state contingent upon the heading the broker has chosen. It is suggested that long position that is upward positions are substantially more superior to the primary short position that is descending position.

The Con: the main poor and awful section has the opportunity to get going the other way to the trade.....

DIFFERENCE BETWEEN SWING TRADING AND OTHER TYPES OF TRADING

Day Trading versus Swing Trading: What's the Difference?

Day Trading versus Swing Trading: An Overview

Dynamic merchants frequently bunch themselves into two camps: the informal investors and the swing brokers. Both look to benefit from transient stock developments (versus long haul ventures), however which exchanging technique is the better one? Here are the upsides and downsides of day exchanging as opposed to swing exchanging, and the significant contrasts between the two.

Day exchanging, as the name proposes, includes making many exchanges a solitary day, in view of specialized examination and modern outlining frameworks. The informal investor's goal is to bring home the bacon from exchanging stocks, products, or monetary forms, by making little benefits on various exchanges and topping misfortunes on unrewarding exchanges. Informal investors regularly don't keep any positions or possess any protections medium-term.

Day exchanging includes an extremely one of a kind range of abilities that can be hard to ace. Investopedia's Become a Day Trader course gives a top to bottom review of day exchanging, total with over five hours of on-request video. During the course, you will take in everything from request types to specialized examination strategies to augment your hazard balanced returns.

Day Trading

The greatest bait of day exchanging is the potential for fantastic benefits. However, this may just be a likelihood for the uncommon person who has every one of the attributes, for example, definitiveness, control, and constancy, required to turn into a fruitful informal investor.

The U.S. Protections and Exchange Commission (SEC) calls attention to that "days brokers regularly endure budgetary misfortunes in their first long periods of exchanging, and numerous never graduate to benefit making status." While the SEC alerts that informal investors should just hazard cash they can stand to lose, actually numerous informal investors cause enormous misfortunes on obtained monies, either through margined exchanges or capital acquired from family or different sources. These misfortunes may reduce their day exchanging profession as well as put them in generous obligation.

The informal investor works alone, free from the impulses of corporate fat cats. He can have an adaptable working calendar, get some much needed rest at whatever point required, and work at his own pace, in contrast to somebody on the corporate treadmill.

Informal investors need to contend with high-recurrence brokers, speculative stock investments, and other market experts who burn through millions to pick up exchanging points of interest. In this condition, an informal investor has minimal decision yet to spend intensely on an exchanging stage, graphing programming, cutting edge PCs, and so forth. Progressing costs incorporate expenses for getting live value statements and commission costs that can include in view of the volume of exchanges.

Long-lasting informal investors love the rush of setting their brains against the market and different experts all day every day. The adrenaline surge from quick fire exchanging is something relatively few dealers will admit to, yet it is a major factor in their choice to bring home the bacon from exchanging. It's dicey these sorts of individuals would be substance going through their days selling gadgets or poring over numbers in an office work space.

To truly cause a to go at it, a dealer must stop his normal everyday employment and surrender his enduring regularly scheduled check. From that point on, the informal investor must depend altogether without anyone else expertise and endeavors to produce enough benefit to take care of the tabs and appreciate a not too bad way of life.

Day exchanging is unpleasant as a result of the need to watch various screens to spot exchanging openings, and after that demonstration rapidly to misuse them. This must be done for a long time, and the prerequisite for such a high level of center and focus can regularly prompt burnout.

For some employments in money, having the correct degree from the correct college is an essential only for a meeting. Day exchanging, interestingly, doesn't require costly instruction from an Ivy League school. While there are no formal instructive necessities for turning into an informal investor, courses in specialized investigation and mechanized exchanging might be useful.

Swing Trading

Swing exchanging depends on distinguishing swings in stocks, wares, and monetary forms that occur over a time of days. A swing exchange may take a couple of days to half a month to work out. In contrast to an informal investor, a swing dealer isn't probably going to make exchanging a full-time vocation.

Anybody with information and speculation capital can have a go at swing exchanging. As a result of the more drawn out time period (from days to weeks instead of minutes to hours), a swing merchant shouldn't be stuck to his PC screen throughout the day. He can even keep up a different all day work (as long as he isn't checking exchanging screens all the time at work).

Exchanges for the most part need time to work out. Keeping an exchange for an advantage open for a couple of days or weeks may bring about higher benefits than exchanging and out of a similar security on numerous occasions a day.

Since swing exchanging as a rule includes positions held in any event medium-term, edge necessities are higher. Most extreme influence is typically multiple times one's capital. Contrast this and day exchanging where edges are multiple times one's capital.

The swing dealer can set stop misfortunes. While there is a danger of a quit being executed at a troublesome value, it beats the steady observing of every single vacant position that are an element of day exchanging.

Likewise with any style of exchanging, swing exchanging can likewise bring about significant misfortunes. Since swing dealers hold their situations for longer than informal investors, they likewise risk bigger misfortunes.

Since swing exchanging is rarely an all day work, there is considerably less shot of burnout because of stress. Swing dealers as a rule have a customary activity or another wellspring of pay from which they can counterbalance or relieve exchanging misfortunes.

Swing exchanging should be possible with only one PC and traditional exchanging devices. It doesn't require the best in class innovation of day exchanging.

Key Differences

Day exchanging and swing exchanging each have points of interest and disadvantages. Neither one of the strategies is superior to the next, and brokers ought to pick the methodology that works best for their aptitudes, inclinations, and way of life. Day exchanging is more qualified for people who are energetic about exchanging full time and have the three Ds: definitiveness, control, and industriousness (essentials for fruitful day exchanging).

Day exchanging achievement likewise requires a propelled comprehension of specialized exchanging and outlining. Since day exchanging is serious and distressing, merchants ought to have the option to remain quiet and control their feelings enduring an onslaught. At last, day exchanging includes hazard—merchants ought to be set up to now and again leave with 100 percent misfortunes.

Swing exchanging, then again, doesn't require such a considerable arrangement of attributes. Since swing exchanging can be embraced by anybody with some venture capital and doesn't require full-time consideration, it is a feasible alternative for brokers who need to keep their all day employments, yet in addition fiddle with the business sectors. Swing brokers ought to likewise have the option to apply a mix of essential and specialized investigation, as opposed to specialized examination alone.

Nugget

Day exchanging, as the name recommends, includes making many exchanges a solitary day, in light of specialized examination and modern outlining frameworks.

Swing exchanging depends on recognizing swings in stocks, wares, and monetary forms that happen over a time of days.

Neither one of the strategies is superior to the next, and merchants ought to pick the methodology that works best for their abilities, inclinations, and way of life.

More on day trading and swing trading

Day exchanging and swing exchanges share two things for all intents and purpose. The two styles of exchanging would like to profit from short moves in the market. They are not for the swoon of heart. To counterbalance the hazard, obviously, there is additionally the probability of extraordinary returns! There is actually nothing that looks at to the fervor of finishing an exceptionally effective exchange. A portion of these exchanges will a minutes ago and some up to a few days. By and by I appreciate day exchanging, swing exchanges are utilized less yet at the same time hold extraordinary benefit potential.

Day exchanging and swing exchanges are distinctive in that swing exchanges are less adaptable. Day exchanging defenders get out toward the finish of consistently however are regularly doing various exchanges every day. One of the qualities of this is knowing where you remain at the end of every day. Swing exchanges may complete in a day or more, yet are similarly prone to keep going for a couple of days and over the span of an exchange there are bound to be more good and bad times in productivity. There is potential to procure more from each swing exchange, however there are dangers. Day exchanging and swing exchanging likely could be your pass to stopping the normal everyday employment If you so want.

Day exchanging has no medium-term dangers, as long as all exchanges are shut before the market close, swing exchanges are increasingly defenseless to news or financial atmosphere during the exchanging day or around evening time. This news can have a negative effect on your situation, outside the ability to control of the swing exchange framework. Day exchanging or swing exchanging without a framework will undoubtedly be unbeneficial.

Day exchanging or swing exchanging frameworks start at $2000 and go up from that point. There is a great deal of assortment in the methodology various brokers take to build up a triumphant framework. How you make your framework for exchanging can be a genuine blend of ways of thinking, yet the most significant thing is to adhere to your framework. Up Or down market bearing has no effect there are in every case huge open doors in day exchanging and swing exchanges an assortment of business sectors.

It is conceivable to exchange a couple of stocks all the time, as long as they adhere to your foreordained arrangement of standards for exchange signals. Exchanging a similar rundown of stocks has the additional impetus that you start to discover what a stock is probably going to do when diverse news or monetary components happen. If you have a solid stock pick asset to begin with, it encourages you to screen out the terrible and discover new stocks.

Scalping versus Swing Trading: The Difference To Spot

Scalping versus Swing Trading: An Overview

Many take an interest in the securities exchanges, some as financial specialists, others as dealers. Contributing is executed considering a long haul see—years or even decades. Exchanging, in the mean time, moves to pocket gains all the time.

A typical strategy for recognizing one sort of dealer from another is the timeframe for which a broker holds a stock—a change which can extend from a couple of moments to months or even years.

The most prominent exchanging systems incorporate day exchanging, swing exchanging, scalping, and position exchanging. Picking a style which suits your very own exchanging personality is fundamental for long haul achievement. This article spreads out the contrasts between a scalping procedure and a swing exchanging system.

Nugget

Scalping and swing exchanging are two of the more famous transient contributing systems utilized by dealers.

Scalping includes making several exchanges day by day which positions are held quickly, now and then only seconds; all things considered, benefits are little, however the hazard is additionally diminished.

Swing exchanging utilizes specialized examination and diagrams to pursue and benefit off patterns in stocks; the time span is middle of the road term, regularly a couple of days to half a month.

Scalping Methodology

Scalping methodology targets minor changes in intra-day stock value development, every now and again entering and leaving all through the exchanging session, to manufacture benefits.

Regularly named a subtype of the day exchanging strategy, scalping includes various exchanges of exceptionally short holding periods from a couple of moments to minutes. Since positions are held for such brief periods, gains on a specific exchange (or benefits per exchange) are little; thus, hawkers do various exchanges—into the hundreds during a normal exchanging day—to assemble benefit. Constrained time presentation to the market lessens hawker chance.

Hawkers are fast, only from time to time embracing a specific example. Hawkers go short in one exchange, at that point long in the following; little open doors are their objectives. Ordinarily working around the offer ask spread—purchasing on the offer and selling at ask—hawkers misuse the spread for benefit. Such chances to effectively adventure are more typical than huge moves, as even genuinely still markets observer minor developments.

Hawkers more often than not pursue brief period graphs, for example, 1-minute outlines, 5-minute diagrams, or exchange based tick graphs, to study value development of and accept approaches certain exchanges.

Hawkers look for sufficient liquidity for its similarity with the recurrence of exchanging. Access to precise information (quote framework, live feed) just as the capacity to quickly execute exchanges is a need for these merchants. High commissions will in general lessen benefit with successive purchasing and selling, as they increment expenses of performing exchanges, so immediate agent access is commonly liked.

Scalping is most appropriate for the individuals who can commit time to the business sectors, remain centered, and act quickly. It's generally said that anxious individuals make great hawkers as they will in general exit from an exchange when it winds up beneficial. Scalping is for the individuals who can deal with pressure, settle on snappy choices, and act in like manner.

Your time period impacts what exchanging style is best for you; hawkers make many exchanges every day and must remain stuck to the business sectors, while swing dealers make less exchanges and can check in less as often as possible.

The methodology of swing exchanging includes distinguishing the pattern, at that point playing inside it. For instance, swing brokers would more often than not pick an emphatically inclining stock after a redress or combination, and just before it's prepared to rise once more, they would exit subsequent to taking some benefit. Such purchasing and selling techniques are rehashed to harvest gains.

In cases wherein stocks fall through help, merchants move to the opposite side, going short. Ordinarily, swing merchants are "pattern supporters," if there is an upswing, they go long, and if the general pattern is towards the drawback, they could go short. Swing exchanges stay open from a couple of days to half a month (close term)— in some cases even to months (transitional term), however regularly enduring just a couple of days.

Regarding time period, persistence required, and potential returns, swing exchanging falls between day exchanging and pattern exchanging. Swing dealers utilize specialized examination and graphs which show value activities, helping them find best purposes of passage and exit for gainful exchanges. These merchants study obstruction and backing, utilizing Fibonacci expansions incidentally joined with different examples and specialized pointers. Some unpredictability is solid for swing exchanging as it offers ascend to circumstances.

Swing merchants keep up cautiousness for a capability of more prominent gains by enjoying less stocks, keeping business expenses low.

The methodology functions admirably for those incapable to remain stuck fulltime to the business sectors, keeping a moment by moment track of things. Low maintenance brokers who set aside effort to look at what's going on during work interims regularly decide on this system. Pre-market and post-advertise audits are vital to fruitful swing exchanging, as is tolerance with medium-term possessions. Hence, it's not for the individuals who get on edge in such circumstances.

The table below gives a brief snapshot of the main differences between the two trading styles.

	Scalp Trading	Swing Trading
Holding Period	A few seconds to minutes, never overnight	A few days to weeks, even months at times; most commonly held for few days
Number of Trades	Can be hundreds during a day	A few
Chart	Tick chart or 1-5 minute charts	Daily or weekly charts
Trader Traits	Vigilance, impatience work well here	Greater patience and precision required to understand trends
Decision-Making Time	Rapid	Fluid
Strategy	Extreme	Moderate
Stress Level	High	Moderate
Profit Target	Small, multiple	Few but large

Tracking	Constant monitoring throughout the trading session	Reasonable monitoring; requires up-to-date info on news and corporate events
Suitability	Not for novice traders	Suitable for all, from beginners to moderate and advanced players

Each style of negotiation has its own set of risks and benefits. There is no `` perfect strategy " for all operators, which is why it is better to choose a business strategy based on your skills, temperament, time you can spend, the size of your account, business experience and your personal risk tolerance.

MARKET PSYCHOLOGY FOR
SWING TRADING

It is genuine you can download an entire host of web recordings, book recordings and PDFs that will give you instances of swing exchanging, principles to pursue and Heiken-Ashi diagrams to assemble. However, what they regularly won't let you know is the means by which to rationally respond when your swing exchanging system doesn't work.

All things considered, you ought to think about the accompanying three hints:

Have an arrangement and stick to it – There will be highs and lows, that is the very idea of purchasing and selling in the business sectors. In any case, let the maths manage those high points and low points, don't give your feelings a chance to disrupt everything. Choosing when to sell can immediately turn into an enthusiastic choice when you have your entire weeks returns on hold. Along these lines, figure a methodology and afterward stick to it strictly.

This is a 24 hour market and is the world's biggest investment marketplace.
The huge size of the markets allows traders to open and close transactions quickly, to lock in profits and minimize losses.

Currency markets are volatile and therefore a short-term trading method, such as currency exchange, can be equally profitable.
The volatile mobile market is crucial for stock trading.
This volatility means a lot of potential opportunities offered to currency traders.

Low transaction costs that were once reserved for large institutions, now each operator can receive spreads of 3 to 5 pips, which means that short-term trade is viable for any operator

Although currencies show long-term trends, there are many profitable exchange opportunities within them.
These shorter trends last for days and weeks and regularly offer currency trading with low risk and high rewards. Psychology is easy to learn.
Many traders lack patience and want quick action and that's exactly what you get by trading currencies.

Forex swing trading offers numerous exchanges on a regular basis and you do not need the patience of a long-term trend follower.

Swing operations tend to win or lose quickly, which is why the operator is interested, motivated, disciplined and focused.

Battle dread by decreasing danger – Everyone's craving for hazard is unique. So discover chance parameters that suit. For instance, you might need to begin by not gambling over 2% of your record size on a solitary exchange. This is something no tutor can instruct you. Just through long periods of training will you realize where your own cutoff points are.

Think long haul – Too numerous dealers fixates on the last exchange or the following. Try not to stress If you simply lost on gold fates. Rather, consider your long haul benefit rate and number cruncher. As Bruce Kovner relevantly called attention to, "If you customize misfortunes, you can't exchange."

Swing Trading Top Tips

Indeed, even the absolute best forex books forget about a portion of the top tips and mysteries of swing exchanging, including:

Use the news – Markets are continually moving in response to news occasions. Numerous assets, for example, Yahoo Finance and CNBC will give advertise investigation and critique, utilizing volume, value activity and week after week outlines. In this way, utilized effectively, the news could enable you to feature potential alternatives and profit stocks to watch out for, for instance. It could likewise enable you to design your entrances and exits.

Learn constantly – As Paul Tudor Jones broadly stated: "The key to being fruitful from an exchanging viewpoint is to have an inexhaustible and an undying and ravenous hunger for data and information." There is an abundance of data accessible to support you create successful cryptographic money and forex techniques. Video instructional exercises, for instance, can help show you Gann procedures and how to begin utilizing week after week somewhere down in the cash choices. They can likewise run you through pointers for your MT4 stage and the setting up of every day stock cautions.

Locate the correct dealer and trade – Everyone has various needs and needs, so while one crypto swing merchant might be best off on Gdax or Binance, an exceptionally dynamic forex swing broker might need to consider Dailyfx. Note they are likewise in excess of a spot to consider statements and trade protections. They can enable you to construct a various watchlist, portfolio, thus significantly more.

Keep a Journal – Keeping an Excel diary can demonstrate precious. Essentially note down value, date, position size and an explanation behind passage and leave focuses. This could enable you to perceive any reason why your breakouts plan for money sets doesn't chip away at week after week graphs, for instance.

The amount Money Can You Make?

Swing exchanging profits depend completely for the dealer. For instance, take utilized ETFs versus stocks, some will yield liberal comes back with the previous while flopping wretchedly with the last mentioned, in spite of the two exchanges being moderately comparative.

It will likewise halfway rely upon the methodology you take. A few people will laud MACD pointers while others use a NMA framework. Much the same as some will depend on utilizing candle outlining with help and obstruction levels, while some will exchange on the news.

The key is to discover a system that works for you and around your timetable. See our procedures page to have the subtleties of figuring an exchanging plan clarified.

Last Thoughts

In spite of the fact that being diverse to day exchanging, audits and results recommend swing exchanging might be a clever framework for novices to begin with. This is on the grounds that the intraday exchange many protections can demonstrate excessively furious. While swing merchants will see their profits inside two or three days, keeping inspiration levels high. Simultaneously versus long haul exchanging, swing exchanging is short enough to avoid interruption.

What's more, prerequisites are low. You need a money market fund and some capital, however from that point onward, you can discover all the assistance you need from online masters to attempt to return benefits. Moreover, swing exchanging can be successful in a colossal number of business sectors.

However, in spite of the fact that figuring out how to begin swing exchanging as low maintenance or all day occupation might be moderately clear, your capital is in danger. Along these lines, alert must be taken consistently.

If exchanging appears to be disappointing and hard to you, don't stress, you are not the only one. Numerous brokers, if not most, start their exchanging professions with elevated objectives and a full tank of expectation, however those things can blur rapidly If you aren't moving toward the market from the right 'edge'.

At Learn To Trade The Market, we take the view that whether a retail dealer (like you or I) makes steady progress in the market depends intensely on which strategy the broker employments. In other words, we accept If you are exchanging with an inappropriate approach, it is highly unlikely you will ever profit, regardless of whether you're doing everything else right.

Exchanging achievement is the final product of getting the "3 M's" correct; Method, Mindset and Money Management. You can't prevail with just two of the three; you should have every one of the three under control.

In this exercise, I need to concentrate on the main M; the Method that will give you the most obvious opportunity to prevail at exchanging. You have to comprehend which strategy is the best, why it is the best and how you can ace it, so we should begin...

Swing Trading: The retail broker's just genuine possibility

I won't mislead you; as a retail Forex merchant, or a retail dealer of any market truly, there are numerous 'powers' neutralizing you, which you may or not have known about as of not long ago. To be completely forthright with you, you are a one-man (or lady) group when you're a dealer, and except if you approach incredibly huge totals of cash/the capacity to withstand huge drawdowns, you won't keep going long If you don't utilize the correct exchanging technique.

The enormous players in the market, similar to banks, flexible investments, and so on know where littler retail brokers put in their requests and what they normally 'do' in the market (purchase breakouts, day-exchange, and so forth.). They know all the little clock systems and in all honesty, they appreciate taking your cash each day in the market. You can't make due without a stop misfortune, yet they can, or possibly they can for any longer than you or I and this is the reason day exchanging is hazardous; on the grounds that merchants put extremely little/tight stop misfortunes on their positions they frequently get halted out by ordinary every day value vacillations in the market.

I'm not going to state that your representative 'needs you to lose', however I think saying they need you to day-exchange is a reasonable appraisal. For what reason do they need you to day-exchange you inquire? All things considered, for one you will produce a great deal of charges as spread installments or commissions, and two, you will lose a ton of exchanges for the explanation I talked about in the past passage. To put it plainly, day-exchanging is a trick's down that sucks individuals in by engaging their eager/fretful want to make 'quick cash'.

On the far edge of the exchanging scale, we have position exchanging or contributing, this is essentially long haul purchase and hold procedures that while they may satisfy when you are prepared to resign, they are not reasonable for anybody hoping to bring home the bacon as a dealer, similar to you and I.

That carries us to what I call the exchanging 'sweet spot'; swing exchanging. If you don't as of now have the foggiest idea about, this is what swing exchanging is: Swing Trading is a strategy for specialized investigation to enable you to spot solid directional moves in the market that keep going by and large, two to six days. Swing exchanging permits singular dealers like us to abuse the solid transient moves made by enormous institutional brokers who can't move all through the market as fast.

What is a 'swing point' in the market?

To place this in a little less complex terms, I'm expecting you have taken a gander at an essential value diagram previously. If you have, you most likely saw that business sectors don't move in straight lines for extremely long. Rather, cost will 'swing' from high to depressed spots in the market. Particularly in a slanting business sector, these diagram swing focuses are basic focuses on a value graph where we can envision a value activity sign to frame at, and that regularly give high-likelihood passages just before a pattern is preparing to continue.

Swing exchanging is the craftsmanship and ability of perusing a value diagram to envision the following 'swing' in the market. I use value activity exchanging procedures to discover high-likelihood passages in the market at these swing focuses, you may see me allude to this as 'purchasing shortcoming's or 'purchasing the dunks' in a rising business sector and 'selling quality' or 'selling the meetings' in a falling business sector. This wording alludes to the general methodology that a swing dealer utilizes; purchasing as a market tumbles down and ideally purchasing the swing depressed spot (or near it) inside an up-slanting business sector, the inverse would be the situation for a down pattern obviously.

Different reasons why you ought to turn into a swing merchant

Since we've talked about what swing exchanging is and the principle motivation behind why you have to learn it and make it your exchanging strategy, we should examine a portion of different advantages of it.

Day by day graphs

As I've expounded on finally in different articles; when you exchange the day by day graph time allotment as a swing broker does, you are receiving numerous rewards contrasted with those poor spirits who still think scalping a 5-minute outline is the way to progress.

Piece

Try not to be tricked by the showcasing and contrivance exchanging frameworks out there. If you've been around the exchanging obstruct a couple of times as of now you most likely hear what I'm saying here. There are a great deal of guarantees and certifications out there in the exchanging scene, yet the inquiry you ought to posture isn't about assurances however about the technique itself. Is the strategy really going to encourage me to comprehend a value graph and how to get enormous moves in the market? Is it really going to show me how to exchange appropriately? These are simply the sorts of inquiries you should pose to yourself about any exchanging framework or instruction you are thinking about, in light of the fact that these are ones that issue. Try not to fall prey to enormous cases of quick cash and completely computerized exchanging robots; recollect, If it sounds unrealistic, it most likely is.

Swing Trading In Forex – The Steps To Thread Swing Trading Success and Beyond

Swing exchanging forex is easy to do and it's an extraordinary route for beginner brokers to begin exchanging - it's additionally fun and an incredible method to heap up huge benefits. We should see swing exchanging forex and 4 straightforward strides to enable you to succeed.

Here are the stages you have to make swing exchanging a gainful piece of your general forex exchanging technique.

1. Substantial Support and Resistance

You have to spot it and use it to spot exchanges.

By and large search for at any rate 3 trial of help or opposition.

Tests that occur in time spans that are wide separated, will in general be increasingly substantial and keeping in mind that 3 is at least tests, tests should there are as much as possible.

When you have spotted trial of help and obstruction, at that point its opportunity to execute your exchanging signal.

2. Affirm

The key with any type of exchanging and swing exchanging forex is the same, isn't to just exchange into help and opposition - this wont work.

Why?

Since - you are basically trusting or speculating the levels will hold.

Trusting and speculating, are not a decent method to look for benefits in any endeavor and swing exchanging forex is the same.

You have to affirm that the levels are going to hold and this implies utilizing energy oscillators.

These can be utilized to quantify moves in force of cost.

For instance, if costs move towards opposition and dismiss with value energy on your side, you have the chance to execute your exchanging sign line with this move and have the chances on your side.

You're not foreseeing or trusting - you are seeing the truth of value change on your forex graphs and following up on the truth.

Affirming a turn is a basic piece of swing exchanging achievement.

So what pointers would it be a good idea for you to use for demonstrating force shifts?

A Great couple of pointers to begin with are:

The stochastic and the Relative Strength Index (RSI) There not by any means the only ones yet an incredible spot to begin - so find them.

3. Stop and Target

Your stop ought to be behind the degree of help or obstruction and you ought to have a benefit target.

When you are swing exchanging forex you are looking for littler FX benefits and they can vanish rapidly, so have an objective to take benefits sooner than the vast majority i.e before the content of the following level.

When you hit your objective bank it.

The closer the exchange goes to the following level, the more the chances of backlash against you are - so bank early.

4. Shop Rates

If you are long haul forex pattern following the expense of business is low as you are exchanging rarely and have greater benefits per exchange.

With swing exchanging forex, you are exchanging all the more regularly and pips mount up, so search around and search for 2 pips on the majors.

Another significant point to remember when swing exchanging is:

You need fluid markets so stock with the significant monetary forms such euro, yen and pound, despite the fact that you can exchange the Australian and Canadian dollar too.

The Best Form Of Trading For Novices

Swing exchanging is incredible for beginners, as it requires less tolerance and order than long haul pattern following.

Benefits and misfortunes come rapidly and you needn't bother with the persistence to sit on patterns for quite a long time or months on end.

Swing exchanging forex should be possible utilizing simply essential help, obstruction a couple of energy markers.

The market is 24 hours and the largest investment market in the world.

The large size of the market allows operators to quickly open and close transactions, freeze profits and minimize losses.

2. Volatility

Currency markets are volatile and therefore a short-term trading method, such as currency exchange, can be equally profitable.

The volatile mobile market is crucial for stock trading. This volatility means a lot of potential opportunities offered to currency traders.

3. Transaction costs

Low transaction costs that were once reserved for large institutions, now each operator can receive spreads of 3 to 5 pips, which means that short-term trade is viable for any operator
This straightforward strategy can lead you to cash exchanging achievement.

While the above sounds a basic framework, remember straightforward strategies work best and are undeniably more powerful than muddled forex exchanging frameworks, as they are progressively vigorous and have less components to break.

Forex Swing exchanging rushes to learn, is fun and energizing and best of all can make you huge forex benefits. So If you are exchanging forex, consider swing exchanging and you perhaps happy you did.

Swing Trading Systems - Buying One For
Long Term Profits

Swing Trading is fun, energizing and can be entirely productive and is probably the most effortless type of exchanging for a beginner to ace.

Swing exchanging frameworks profit by the motions experienced in the stock costs. In this style of exchanging, the profits on a stock can be picked up in couple of days or inside up to 14 days. Merchants utilizing this style can use on the transient stock developments without dreading any hardened challenge from the huge players in the market. Swing exchanging frameworks are most appropriate for the at-home or low maintenance brokers. These brokers need more time for continually observing the stock costs like the informal investors. They can just bear to look out for the market progress once in a day or week. They need to depend on the administrations of specialist firms, who tell them about the value changes utilizing email alarms and bulletins.

Huge exchanging firms or offices can't exchange their stocks at a fast pace, attributable to the mass size of the possessions. They in this way don't embrace swing exchanging frameworks as their pillar. Rather they use the exchanging framework at times to acquire modest quantities of benefit. Informal investors likewise avoid this style of exchanging in light of their inclination of not clutching a stock for over a day. They exchange their stocks inside minutes or hours. The low maintenance dealers and the newcomers in the market generally lean toward swing-exchanging frameworks. The low dangers and speedy returns structure an alluring mix for these merchants.

Swing exchanging frameworks are best utilized in a steady market. Here, the stock costs demonstrate a general example of variety, the vast majority of which can be anticipated. Frequently these little varieties are overlooked continuously merchant and the long haul financial specialists. A swing broker then again observes heaps of chances. He/she exchanges on stocks having minor changes. In the event of a bullish or bearish market, the stock costs will in general move a solitary way either up or down. They don't vary. Swing exchanging frameworks thusly can't be utilized in such markets. In the steady market, the best wager for the swing merchant is the blue-chip stocks. These are the stocks that are effectively exchanged generally trades. Supplies of huge organizations ordinarily show significant varieties, which convert into more prominent benefits for the swing dealer.

There are many swing exchanging frameworks that are sold by merchants through digital books and programming, and courses or obviously you can manufacture your own.

Lets take a gander at picking a swing exchanging framework that can be you some extraordinary capital additions - so what makes an effective swing exchanging framework?

Allow's find to out.

Right off the bat we should give our meaning of swing exchanging

The object of a swing exchanging methodology is to profit from the middle of the road swings inside the more drawn out term patterns and these normally keep going for a couple of days or half a month - this isn't day exchanging!

You can't profit day exchanging as there is no solid information - don't as well attempt.

Alright we should take a gander at getting one from a merchant and focuses to consider.

Here are a few focuses to think about when buying a trading system from a vendor:

1. Understand the rationale

In the event that are swing trading forex stocks, or prospects you have to understand EXACTLY how the methodology works and why it will be fruitful.

You should understand why the system will work since you will must have the discipline to follow it through losing periods and this solitary originates from understanding and confidence.

So If you buy a forex swing trading system don't follow it aimlessly, understand every little thing about it. You need the discipline to follow a trading system through losing periods, or you have no method in any case.

Swing trading is basically basic and the method ought to be easy to understand and apply.

2. Does it suit your trading personality?

Swing trading systems change as far as the dangers they take and the drawdowns they bring about - make sure that you buy a swing trading system that suits your personality and your hazard resistance.

3. The track record

While a track record doesn't ensure future profitability, it gives you confidence in its ability to make cash and what it is prepared to do.

Search for a continuous track record of benefits over a multi year time of trading.

Try not to believe speculative track records these are finished knowing the closing prices and truly If you know the closing prices its easy to make a benefit!

4. The vendor

Find out however much as could reasonably be expected about the vendor and their trading experience - numerous systems are sold by bombed dealers or showcasing people, who just make up a speculative track record, so be careful before buying.

Search for an unconditional promise if conceivable. This will give you the solace that you will recover your cash if the swing trading system you are being sold doesn't satisfy the vendors claims.

Swing trading is incredible for fledgling dealers as it gives customary exchanges and a lot of activity while hitting the exceptional yield generally safe trading openings.

Trading openings additionally don't take long to finish and the outcome is immediately known - ideally in the swing merchant's support!

There are some incredible swing trading systems you can buy and get the correct one and you could be making some extraordinary customary capital increases from your system - Just be cautious in your choice and follow the above tips.

Forex Swing Trading - Swing Trade Your Way To Regular Profit

The ascent of online forex trading implies that anybody can swing trade for transient benefits, Its not just profitable, its easy to learn, great enjoyment and that is the thing that trading ought to be.

Forex swing trading on the web gives the ideal market to the methodology of swing trading.

So for what reason are currency markets the ideal for swing trading?

Lets above all else characterize what forex swing trading really is

Forex Swing trading expects to distinguish middle of the road swings in value, that can last from anyplace from a couple of days, to half a month.

This isn't day trading - day trading has no solid information as the period is to short and you cannot make cash.

Swing trading here methods as yet seeing brief timeframe outlines, yet the information is dependable enough for you to get the chances in support of you.

The following conditions make FOREX swing trading conceivably such a rewarding method for trading

1. Liquidity

Every day the worldwide forex markets see trillions of dollars executed.

This is a 24 hour advertise and is the world's greatest speculation commercial center.

The enormous size of the markets enables traders to open and close exchanges rapidly, to secure benefits and limit misfortunes.

2. Instability

Currency markets are unstable and this is the reason a momentary trading method, for example, forex swing trading can be so profitable.

An unstable moving business sector is fundamental for swing trading.

This instability implies countless potential open doors that are exhibited to forex traders.

3. Exchange costs

Low exchange costs that were at one time the protect of huge establishments, presently any trader can get 3 - 5 pip spreads importance momentary trading is reasonable for any trader

Swing exchanges come normally

This is an ideal method for trading for somebody who loves trading.

Forex swing trading is moreover

Easy to learn you can just utilize backing and obstruction lines with some affirming energy pointers. For instance, we utilize just stochastics and

RSI - It's straightforward and a peaceful method for trading and best of all can make enormous benefits with generally safe.

FOREX Swing trading is fun and entirely profitable and that is the manner in which trading ought to be.

THE PRICE ACTION

Value activity is the development of a security's value plotted after some time. Value activity frames the reason for all specialized examination of a stock, item or other resource outline. Some transient merchants depend solely on value activity and the developments and patterns extrapolated from it to settle on exchanging choices. Specialized examination as a training is a subsidiary of value activity since it utilizes past costs in computations that would then be able to be utilized to illuminate exchanging choices.

Nugget

Value activity by and large alludes to the here and there development of a security's cost when it is plotted after some time.

Various looks can be applied to an outline to make inclines in value activity increasingly evident for brokers.

Specialized examination arrangements and diagram examples are gotten from value activity. Specialized investigation devices like moving midpoints are determined from value activity and anticipated into the future to advise exchanges.

What Does Price Action Tell You?

Value activity can be seen and translated utilizing outlines that plot costs after some time. Brokers utilize diverse outline pieces to improve their capacity to spot and translate patterns, breakouts and inversions. Numerous dealers use candle outlines since they help better envision value developments by showing the open, high, low, and close qualities with regards to up or down sessions.

Candle examples, for example, the Harami cross, overwhelming example and three white troopers are altogether instances of outwardly deciphered value activity. There are a lot more candle arrangements that are created off value activity to set up a desire for what will come straightaway. These equivalent developments can apply to different kinds of outlines, including point and figure diagrams, box graphs, box plot, etc.

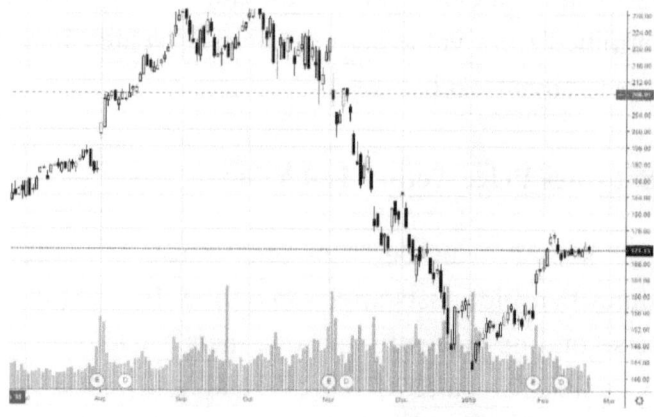

In addition to the visual formations on the chart, many technical analysts use price action data when calculating technical indicators. The goal is to find order in the sometimes seemingly random movement of price. For example, an ascending triangle pattern formed by applying trendlines to a price action chart may be used to predict a potential breakout since the price action indicates that bulls have attempted a breakout on several occasions and have gained momentum each time.

How to Use Price Action

Price action is not generally seen as a trading tool like an indicator, but rather the data source off which all the tools are built. Swing traders and trend traders tend to work most closely with price action, eschewing any fundamental analysis in favor of focusing solely on support and resistance levels to predict breakouts and consolidation. Even these traders must pay some attention to additional factors beyond the current price, as the volume of trading and the time periods being used to establish levels all have an impact on the likelihood of their interpretations being accurate.

Tips That Will Make You a Better Swing Trader Regarding Price Action

Price action for swing traders is the craft of seeing individual candles to determine the likely heading of a stock - without utilizing any specialized pointers.

Eventually, examining price action reveals to you who is in charge of a stock. It likewise reveals to you who is losing control: the buyers or the venders. When you can determine this, you can pinpoint inversions in a stock and make cash.

Learn the price action tips on this page and I promise you that you will be a superior swing trader.

We should start.

Tip #1. Recognize backing and resistance levels

This is an easy decision. Distinguishing backing and resistance levels is one of the main things you learn in specialized examination. It is the most significant part of outline reading. Be that as it may, what number of traders truly focus on it? Relatively few. Most are excessively bustling taking a gander at Stochastics, MACD, and other nonsense.

A few traders imagine that a help or resistance level is a particular price. Wrong. It's a zone on a stock outline. Let me give you a model.

The areas that I have highlighted are the correct support and resistance levels. Often times you will hear traders say something like this: "The support level for XYZ stock is $28.76." This is wrong. It's an area - not a specific price.

Tip #2. Analyze swing points

Swing points (some call them "pivot points") are those areas on a stock chart where important short term reversals take place. But not all swing points are created equal. If fact, your decision to buy a pullback will depend upon the prior swing point. Here is an example:

Look at the area that I have highlighted in green. You may have considered buying this pullback. Now look at the prior swing point high (yellow highlighted). There are two problems with buying this pullback. First, there isn't much room to work with! The distance between the pullback and the prior high is too small. You need more room to run so that you can at least get your stop to break even.

The second problem is this: The prior high (yellow area) is composed of a cluster of candles. This is a strong resistance area! So, it will be very difficult for a stock to break through this area. Instead, look to trade pullbacks where the prior high is only composed of one or two candles.

Tip #3. Look for wide range candles
Wide range candles mark important changes in sentiment on every chart - in every time frame. They mark important turning points and can often be used to identify reversals. Take a look at the following stock chart:

This stock was moving lower in October (highlighted) and then suddenly it dropped more significantly than on previous days. This created the wide range candle and it marked an important turning point (actually the bottom!).

You can also use wide range candles to identify when a stock might reverse. Looking at the same chart...

This stock switched within earlier wide range candles. For what reason would a stock do this? Since the majority of the dealers that passed up "the enormous move" presently have another opportunity to get in. This purchasing weight causes the inversion. Straightforward, huh?

Tip #4. Tight range candles lead to hazardous moves

Limited range candles can likewise disclose to you that an inversion is fast approaching. This low instability condition can prompt touchy moves.

Restricted range candles reveal to you that the past energy has backed off. Purchasers and dealers are in harmony yet in the end one of them will assume responsibility for the stock!

Tip #5. Get and Discover dismissed value levels

On candle graphs, lower or upper shadows on candles more often than not implies that there is a mallet candle design or a meteorite candle design (if the shadow is long enough). Despite the name, these shadows mean a certain something: A value level has been dismissed.

Envision what this sledge light resembled during the day preceding (it turned into a mallet). It was extremely bearish! However, sooner or later during the day, the bulls dismissed the lower value level. I can envision the bulls saying, "Hello hold up an only a second. You bears have taken this excessively far. This stock is worth a lot more than the value that you moved it to."

What's more, the purchasing starts.

Tip #6. Always Become familiar with the half standard

How might you tell if a light is noteworthy? Simple. Hope to perceive how far it has moved into the earlier days go. If it moves at any rate half into the earlier days run, at that point it is noteworthy. What's more, it is particularly critical If it closes at any rate half into the earlier days extend. This generally appears on the stock diagram as a piercing candle design or an immersing candle design.

The majority of the significant inversions in this stock happened simply after a flame moved at any rate half into the earlier days extend (some moved considerably more than half).

This idea is incredible to such an extent that I am suspicious of purchasing any pullback except if it moves in any event half into the earlier days extend.

Tip #7. The hole and trap value design

All holes are significant "tells" on any stock diagram. In any case, there is one kind of hole that is particularly significant when examining value activity (and pinpointing inversions). This is known as a hole and snare. This is a stock that holes down at the open yet then shuts the day over the opening cost. It is simpler to see this on an outline...

You can most likely observe what's going on here. The stock holes down at the open. Everybody thinks this stock is going to tank. However, it doesn't! Purchasers come in and move this stock ideal back up. You can take a gander at one of these candles and nearly observe the majority of the confounded faces on other stock merchants!

Tip #8. Measure the profundity of a swing

How far does a stock move into the earlier swing? More than midway or less? The response to these inquiries are significant in light of the fact that it can decide the future heading of the stock.

The value activity moved mostly down (bolt) into the earlier swing (dabbed line). This is great. If it followed more than that, you might need to scrutinize the legitimacy of the move. This is on the grounds that a stock in a solid pattern ought not remember more than most of the way into an earlier swing. It should experience purchasing weight sooner than the midway imprint. What's more, ordinarily stocks will turn around appropriate at the midway imprint.

Tip #9. Back to back up days and sequential down days

Stocks will invert course after back to back up days or down days. Thus, it pays to remember this when you are hoping to purchase or short a stock.

You ought to consistently hope to short a stock after successive up days. Furthermore, you should hope to purchase a stock after sequential down days. This is outlandish for new merchants since they will in general partner a stock going down as "terrible" (which means sell) and a stock going up as "great" (which means purchase). Truth be told, it is the exact inverse!

Tip #10. Area of cost in a pattern

You have heard the platitude, "The pattern is your companion." I state, "The start of a pattern is your companion!" That is on the grounds that the absolute best moves happen at the earliest reference point of a pattern...

This stock broke out (even line) from a twofold base (circumnavigated). Another pattern has started. Along these lines, you need to purchase this stock on the principal pullback (bolt) after the breakout.

Along these lines, there you have it. These value activity tips and deceives will profit in the securities exchange.

You can utilize this data to make your very own exchanging procedures and frameworks. The best part is that once you ace this craftsmanship, you will never need to depend on specialized markers again to settle on exchanging choices.

Becoming a price action trader: Viable steps to Consider

It is safe to say that you are another merchant hoping to gain proficiency with a straightforward exchanging technique? Or on the other hand a prepared merchant attempting to disentangle your exchanging? In the two cases, an appropriate objective is to turn into a value activity dealer.

At its center, value activity exchanging is another gadget in a broker's tool kit. However, the manner in which you learn value activity exchanging can represent the moment of truth your inevitable exchanging profession. It can liken to either well-spent focused on training or a misuse of your time and cash.

Value activity exchanging falls into place without any issues for a few. In any case, for most, it's an unusual scene that is difficult to explore.

Turning into a value activity merchant shouldn't be an arbitrary procedure. You can turn into a value activity merchant with these 5 viable advances.

#1: APPRECIATE PRICE ACTION TRADING FOR WHAT IT IS

Numerous merchants bounce straight into learning value activity. What happens is that they start with confusions, and end with disillusionment.

To have a practical learning venture, acknowledge value activity exchanging for what it is.

The key quality of value activity exchanging is straightforwardness. A distinct spotlight on value gives you what you have to settle on reasonable exchanging choices.

Do you appreciate a basic way to deal with life? Assuming this is the case, you will discover value activity exchanging engaging.

Do you like tinkering with equations and performing measurable tests to maintain a strategic distance from multicollinearity? Provided that this is true, value activity exchanging probably won't be for you.

Another significant note before you start. Value activity doesn't ensure your exchanging achievement. This is on the grounds that exchanging is substantially more than just examination.

Suppose you've been exchanging with markers and an overtrading issue. In the wake of acing value activity, you will exchange with value activity and an overtrading issue. You are overtrading and unrewarding in the two cases.

While value activity may change your market see, it doesn't settle your own issues.

#2: START LEARNING FROM SCRATCH

When you've revised your desires for value activity exchanging, let the learning start.

As referenced, value activity exchanging offers a preferred position since it is a basic methodology. You would prefer not to entangle it from the beginning.

Henceforth, the most ideal approach to learn value activity is to go gradually, from base up.

This means you ought not begin with:

- Head and shoulders
- Inundating candles
- Renko bars
- Point and figure
- And the various ideas with extravagant names
- You should begin with:

- Bar open, close, high, and low
- Bar tail and body (selling and purchasing weight and quality)
- Swing turns (defining moments)
- Ideas of help and obstruction (showcase structure)

With a solid establishment of value activity, you can get modern ideas effectively. You can separate value designs. You can likewise welcome the fundamental rationale of each example and not be stalled by their marks.

#3: REPLACE YOUR TRADING INDICATORS

In the wake of getting a handle on the fundamental value activity instruments, your day of work to value activity exchanging can start.

If you have been utilizing pointers, it will be a test to peel your preferred devices off the value outline. The key is to approach this assignment with an unmistakable framework.

Pursue this framework.

Rundown down the markers you are utilizing.

For every marker, record its motivation.

Would you be able to accomplish a similar reason with value activity?

If you can, evacuate the marker.

Try not to feel that you are evacuating your exchanging markers. Consider it supplanting your pointers with value activity techniques.

For example, you have a 50-period straightforward moving normal on your diagram. You use it to measure the market pattern.

Presently, think about the value activity techniques you've figured out how to decide the pattern. For example pattern lines and market swing structure.

Would you be able to distinguish the market pattern utilizing these techniques?

If your answer is "yes", at that point you can securely evacuate the moving normal.

You probably won't be alright with unadulterated value activity investigation. It's fine to keep the pointer on, yet increment your emphasis on value developments.

After some time, as you sharpen your value activity aptitudes, you will locate the moving normal repetitive.

Notwithstanding, you have to remain centered. Power yourself to utilize value activity as your essential instrument. Allude to the markers just when you're uncertain.

If not, you will be confounded, as you can't choose which apparatus to trust – value activity or marker.

#4: FORM A PRICE ACTION TRADING STRATEGY

With what you've found out about value activity, build your value activity exchanging technique.

Pursue these rules:

Keep it basic. Utilize just the value activity strategies that sound good to you. Try not to attempt to over-burden your cerebrum with new ideas.

Adhere to the kind of exchanges you're utilized to. If you have been exchanging retracements with pointers, at that point stick to exchanging retracements. The main contrast is that you use value activity procedures now.

Keep one pointer, If you wish. Most merchants have a most loved pointer. If you feel shaky exchanging exposed, keep one marker. In any case, recollect that your point is to wean yourself off the marker and not to utilize it as a prop.

This value activity exchanging system is a work-in-progress. In any case, it is a strong launchpad at your cost activity exchanging instruction.

#5: SIMULATE AND FORWARD TEST WITH PRICE ACTION TRADING

We start learning value activity by paying special mind to value examples and market swings. At the end of the day, we start with the study of value activity exchanging.

However, value activity exchanging is additionally a craftsmanship. You can just grow genuine ability through watching the market progressively. Understanding value activity trading.

These five stages aren't enchantment — and you may need to rehash a few stages, however they do work. What's more, If you can remain dirty, you'll remain to benefit from an easier way to deal with exchanging.

Swing Trading Strategies That Work

Does the market consistently appear to move lower after you hit the purchase catch?

Do you wish your exchange will be over soon in light of the fact that you HATE to watch your P&L swing here and there?

Is it true that you are baffled to see the market ALMOST arrived at your objective benefit, however just to do a 180-degree inversion and hit your stop misfortune?

If you said YES to any of the abovementioned, at that point I have the response for you.

Swing exchanging.

Presently you may ponder:

"What is swing exchanging and how can it work?

Try not to stress.

Since in this post, you'll get the hang of all that you have to think about swing exchanging — including 3 swing exchanging techniques that work.

Sounds great?

At that point we should start…

Swing Trading Basics: What is swing exchanging and how can it work

Swing exchanging is an exchanging system that looks to catch a swing (or "one move").

The thought is to suffer as "little agony" as conceivable by leaving your exchanges before the contradicting weight comes in.

This implies you'll book your benefits before the market switch and crash your additions.
Here's an example:

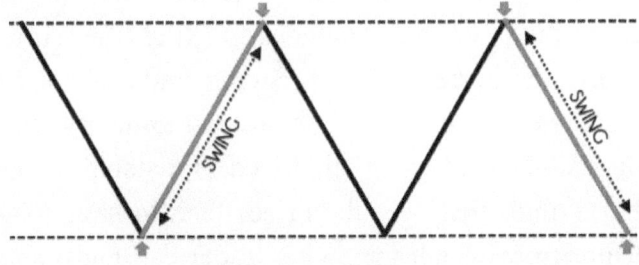

Next, here are the pros & cons when it comes to swing trading…

Pros:

You need not expend hours in front of your monitor because your trades last for days or even weeks
It is doable and suitable for those with a full-time job
Less stress compared to day trading

Cons:
You won't be able to ride trends
You have overnight risk
So far so good?
Then let's move on…

SWING STRATEGIES: CONCEPT

Swing trading is a well known method of benefiting from the short-term price varieties of the stock market. It has earned a notoriety of being a ground-breaking method of boosting profits at lower dangers. The best swing trading strategy includes picking the correct stock and the correct market. Swing traders as a rule pick the stocks that vacillate at extraordinary ends. Swing trading strategy is employed in a stable market, on the grounds that here the prices tend to have minor departure from which the swing trader can underwrite. In a quickly rising or smashing market, swing trading strategy can't be employed.

Newcomers to the stock market regularly pick swing trading attributable to the generally safe and shorter period included. To accomplish higher profits in this short period, the correct swing trading strategy is to trade in stocks of huge organizations. These stocks, ordinarily called huge top stocks, are generally traded on most stock exchanges. Their prices show higher varieties contrasted with other stocks. This converts into more profits for the swing traders. A swing trader may follow a stock during its upward excursion for a couple of days. In the event that the stock inverts its trend, the trader just switches over to another rising stock. The choice of the correct stock hence shapes an indivisible piece of an effective swing trading strategy.

Aside from the choice of stock, the choice of market assumes a key job while settling on a legitimate swing trading strategy. In a market that is on a rising or falling trend, the stock prices for the most part move a solitary way. There isn't quite a bit of a variety by which the swing trader can benefit. The best strategy here is to trade on the long haul premise. A swing trader best works on a stable market, where the list ascends for certain days and falls throughout the following scarcely any days. In spite of the fact that the estimation of significant stocks remains generally the equivalent, the short-term varieties give the much expected chance to the swing trader. The best swing trading strategy is along these lines the best possible choice of the correct stock and right market.

Swing trading methodologies #1: Stuck in a box

Furthermore, a certain something…

The swing trading methodologies I'm going to impart to have "fascinating" names appended to it.

This encourages you understand the trading arrangement better so you realize how to apply it to your trading.

Presently, let me acquaint with you the main swing trading strategy for today…

Stuck in a box.

It's swing trading in a range market on the grounds that the market is "stuck" among Support and Resistance (fairly like a box).

Here's the manner by which it works:

Recognize a range market

Wait at the cost to break underneath Support

In the event that the price breaks beneath Support, at that point wait at a strong cost rejection (a nearby above Support)

In the event that there's a strong price rejection, at that point go long on the following flame open

Set your stop misfortune 1 ATR underneath the flame low and take profits before Resistance

Here's a model:

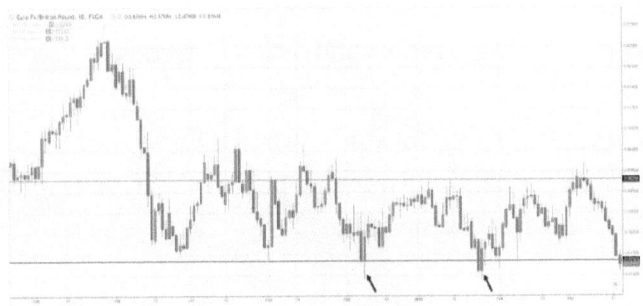

Now you will wonder:
"Why Should I Take Profit Before Resistance?"
Reminder ...
As a swing trader, looking for movement in the market.
Therefore, to ensure a high probability of success, you must leave your business before selling pressure (which is resistance).
Does that make sense?
Well, because we apply that concept to the remaining commercial rocking strategies.

Swing trading systems #2: Catch the wave

This swing trading strategy centers around catching "one move" in a trending market (like a surfer attempting to catch the wave).

The thought here is to enter after the pullback has ended when the trend is probably going to proceed.

In any case...

This doesn't work for a wide range of trends.

Rather, you need to trade trends that have a more profound pullback in light of the fact that there's more "meat" towards the upside.

As a rule, you need to see a pullback at any rate towards the 50-time frame moving normal (MA) or more profound.

Presently, how about we learn how to catch the wave with this swing trading strategy...

Recognize a trend that respects the 50MA

In the event that the market moves toward the moving normal, at that point wait at a bullish cost rejection

In the event that there's a bullish price rejection, at that point go long on next flame

Set your stop misfortune 1 ATR beneath the low and take profits just before the swing high

Here's a model:

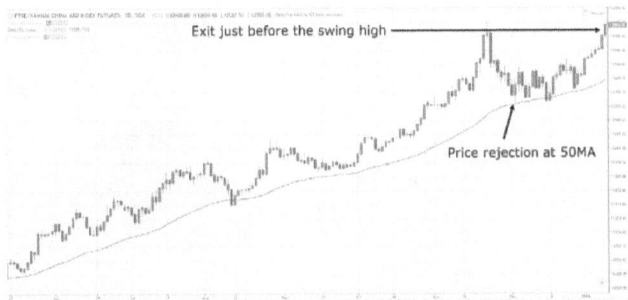

Swing Trading Strategies # 3: Fade The Move

I probably think:

"What does fading mean?"

So ... go against it.

Basically, anti-momentum trading (also known as counter trend).

So if a trader likes to go against the masses, this negotiating strategy is for you.

This is how it works ...

Identify the strong impetus to move toward the Resistance that has the highest precedent

Look for a strong price rebound as the candle forms a powerful teddy bear close by

Go briefly to the next candle and place a stop loss 1 ATR above the peaks

Take advantage of profits before the nearest momentum

Here's an example:

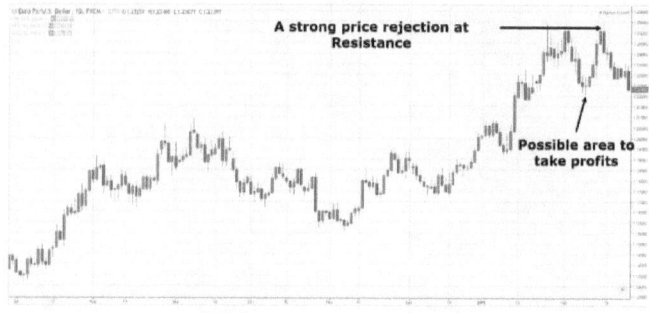

Step by step instructions to manage your trades so you can trade with confidence and conviction

Presently, with trade management, there are 2 different ways you can go about it...

Passive trade management: Active management

1. Passive trade management

For this method, you'll either let the market either hit your stop loss or target benefit — anything between, you'll sit idle.

Ideally, you need to set your stop loss away from the "clamor" of the markets and have an objective benefit inside a sensible reach (before key market structure).

Here are the pros and cons of it...

Pros:

Trading is increasingly loose as your choices become progressively "computerized"

Cons:

You can't exit your trade early despite the fact that the market is giving indications of inversion

Conceivable to see a triumphant trade become a full 1R loss

2. Active management

For this, you'll observe how the market responds and afterward choose whether you need to hold or exit the trade.

Presently, this is significant...

For an active way to deal with work, you should manage your trades on your entrance time period (or higher).

Try not to make the slip-up of overseeing it on a lower time period since you'll alarm yourself out of a trade on each pullback that happens.

Here are the pros and cons of it...

Pros:

You can limit your losses as opposed to getting a full 1R loss

Cons:

Progressively unpleasant

You may exit your trade too early without giving it enough space to run

If active trade management is for you, at that point here are two strategies you can consider:

Moving average

Past bar high/low

Allow me to clarify...

Moving Average

This strategy includes utilizing a moving average pointer to trail your stops.

You'll clutch the trade if the price doesn't break past the moving average.

In the event that it does, at that point you'll exit the trade.

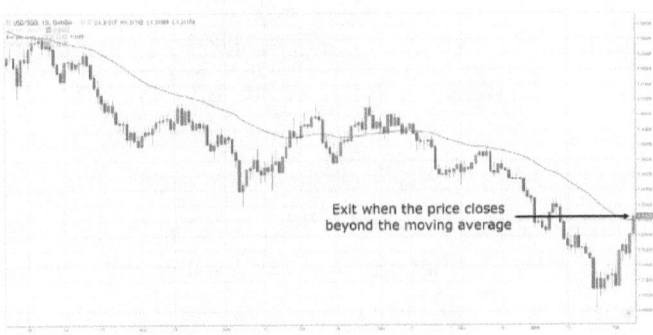

This technique is useful for commercial swing strategies, such as "Catch the Wave", since the moving average acts as a dynamic support and resistance in trendy markets.
Continue ...

Past bar high/low

This method depends on the past bar high/low to trail your stop misfortune.

This implies If you're short, at that point you'll trail your stop misfortune utilizing the past bar high.

If the market breaks and closes above it, at that point you'll leave the exchange (and the other way around).

Confinements of Price Action

Translating value activity is exceptionally emotional. It's normal for two merchants to land at various ends when investigating a similar value activity. One dealer may see a bearish downtrend and another might accept that the value activity demonstrates a potential close term turnaround. Obviously, the timespan being utilized likewise affects what dealers see as a stock can have numerous intraday downtrends while keeping up a month over month upswing. The significant thing to recall is that exchanging forecasts made utilizing value activity on whenever scale are theoretical. The more apparatuses you can apply to your exchanging forecast to affirm it, the better. At last, However, the past value activity of a security is no assurance of future value activity. High likelihood exchanges are as yet theoretical exchanges, which means merchants go out on a limb to gain admittance to the potential prizes.

Swing Trading Stocks

Here are a portion of the contrasts between Swing Trading Stocks and Day Trading. Day Trading is called 'Day Trading' for the conspicuous explanation that it identifies with a specific range of time and Swing Trading Stocks likewise speaks to a specific range of time. The range of time that Swing Trading speaks to is a more drawn out timeframe than day exchanging however a shorter timeframe than somebody who is 'contributing' or in as long as possible. For bookkeeping and expense purposes, anything short of a year is considered 'present moment' exchanging. Anything over a year is considered 'long haul'.

Swing exchanging is an alternate 'style' of exchanging. It suits people that would prefer to be in an exchange longer than an informal investor would. Informal investors only from time to time let an exchange stay impact medium-term. They will enter a position and leave that equivalent situation around the same time. Swing brokers will leave their exchange open for two or three weeks to up to a while.

Swing Trading Stocks Pros and Cons

Similarly as with all things, Swing Trading Stocks has its Good Side and Bad Side

Those that swing exchange stocks will in general accept that they are in a less powerless situation than the positions held by informal investors. In spite of the fact that I can comprehend their manner of thinking, I accept that they are both similarly unsafe relying on the experience, brain research and specialized examination system utilized by the merchant. Everybody assumes that long haul contributing is the most secure wagered yet I don't think so and I can utilize late market movement as a prime case of this. As I would see it, the more drawn out an exchange is presented to the business sectors, the more hazard is apparent. Speculation financiers have persuaded the overall population that contributing is unreasonably muddled for the normal person and that he should leave his cash with the business 'for safety's sake'.

The Pros of Swing Trading Stocks

Less tedious than day exchanging. A merchant is given additional time in the middle of exchanges to play out his/her examination and could pick better entertainers.

An underlying poor section has the opportunity to recuperate and come back to a positive state subordinate upon the bearing the merchant has picked. Long (up) positions will frequently reasonable preferable in this regard over an underlying Short (down) position.

Swing Traders need not be worried about gathering the 'Example Day Trader' prerequisites.

Swing brokers are given more information to examine (time span insightful) than are informal investors. A swing dealer has more trust in his/her exchange in light of the fact that the present pattern is upheld by longer term recorded information.

The Cons of Swing Trading Stocks (twofold edged swords from the Pros recorded previously)

Less tedious than day exchanging. A broker is given additional time in the middle of exchanges to play out his/her investigation and could pick better entertainers.

Con: A Swing Trader can likewise get awful data in with the general mish-mash of their information investigation and pick a less gainful performing stock or a losing stock.

An underlying poor passage has the opportunity to recuperate and come back to a positive state subordinate upon the course the dealer has picked. Long (up) positions will regularly reasonable preferable in this regard over an underlying Short (down) position.

Con: An underlying poor section additionally has the opportunity to continue moving against your exchange.

A swing dealer, informal investor or any 'merchant' must know consistently of what they are doing and what they could anticipate from some random exchange. Here is a concise check rundown of exceptionally essential things to break down before going into an exchange alongside a little tip.

Check your certainty level on the accompanying:

Brain research of the exchange

Is it true that you are responsible for your Fear, Greed, Patience and Desperation? Ensure your swing exchanging plan for all intents and purposes disposes of any of these feelings else you could settle on a hurried choice. Additionally ensure that you are exchanging just expendable money to wipe out urgent basic leadership.

Up (Long) or Down (Short)

Any exchange will return you to the extremely fundamental inquiry that you should reply before entering the exchange. Do you think the stock will go up or down? What investigation has carried you to this end and do you have supporting proof from outside hotspots for your answer? If you can't offer your response some help, at that point your answer might be only a 'speculation' and you should consider not entering the exchange by any means.

Trust in your procedure

Are your specialized markers demonstrated by YOU? Have you utilized them before by paper exchanging or with different exchanges? Have they worked for you? Straightforward Moving Averages and Exponential Moving Averages will in general be one of the most steady specialized markers accessible.

Build up Your Own Profitable Forex Swing Trading Strategy

Swing exchanging is a mainstream exchanging styles which actualized by numerous dealers around the globe. Dealers of securities, outside trade, financial exchange, items and stock records apply this exchanging style to accept exchanging open door accessible available they exchange. Swing exchanging more often than not has an objective to attempt to get 100 of benefit from each exchange. Huge enough, in addition when a dealer can do it reliably, state the person can win two exchanges every week, you can check the benefit potential inside an exchanging month.

Is it feasible for you to be a decent swing broker? Sure you can, it is truly conceivable. Anyway it will rely upon yourself and your exertion. How terrible you need to ace swing exchanging? How huge is your money to execute it? No one but you can respond to these inquiries. Swing exchanging is like other exchanging styles, it has a hazard. However, luckily, swing exchanging systems ordinarily attempt to accomplish great exchanging set up. It implies these procedures regularly have a sensible hazard and reward proportion.

Presently as you are getting increasingly inquisitive on swing exchanging techniques, and If you truly need to build up your very own systems, a choice you can have is finding those methodologies which accessible online as your references. There are some exchanging sites, broker websites and exchanging discussions which present a few instructions and clarifications on swing exchanging procedures and other exchanging styles.

You may likewise get some training materials accessible on book shops, both on the web or disconnected. Nonetheless, when you need to buy any online Forex teacher administrations, if you don't mind ensure that they are genuine ones on the grounds that there are some Forex instructor tricks focusing on amateur and disappoint merchants. They state that they present the best Forex instruction and Forex exchanging techniques however they simply sell pointless items and administrations.

THE REASON WHY MOST
PEOPLE LOSE MONEY

A usually realized actuality is that most forex brokers fall flat. Indeed, it is assessed that 96 percent of forex brokers lose cash and wind up stopping. The forex site DailyFX found that numerous forex brokers show improvement over that, yet new merchants still have an extreme planning making strides in this market. To enable you to make it into that slippery 4 percent of winning merchants, the accompanying rundown demonstrates to you probably the most well-known reasons why forex brokers lose cash.

Become a close acquaintence with the Market

The market isn't something you beat, however something you comprehend and join when a pattern is characterized. Simultaneously, the market is something that can shake you out If you are attempting to get a lot from it with excessively minimal capital. Having the "beating the market" mentality regularly makes merchants exchange too forcefully or conflict with patterns, which is a certain catastrophe waiting to happen.

Low Start-Up Capital

Most cash merchants begin searching for an approach to escape obligation or to profit. It is basic for forex advertisers to urge you to exchange enormous part sizes and exchange utilizing high influence to produce huge profits for a modest quantity of beginning capital.

You should have some cash to profit, and it is workable for you to produce extraordinary profits for restricted capital for the time being. However, with just a modest quantity of capital and outsized hazard in light of too-high influence, you will end up being passionate with each swing of the market's good and bad times and hopping in and out and the most noticeably terrible occasions conceivable.

You can resolve this issue by never exchanging with a too-modest quantity of capital. This is a troublesome issue to get around for somebody that needs to begin exchanging on a shoestring. $1,000 is a sensible add up to beginning off with If you exchange exceptionally little (miniaturized scale parcels or littler). Else, you are simply setting yourself up for potential debacle.

Inability to Manage Risk

Hazard the board is critical to endurance as a forex dealer as throughout everyday life. You can be an extremely gifted broker and still be cleared out by poor hazard the board. Your main occupation isn't to make a benefit, but instead to ensure what you have. As your capital gets exhausted, your capacity to make a benefit is lost.

To neutralize this danger and execute great hazard the executives, put in stop-misfortune requests and move them once you have a sensible benefit. Use parcel measures that are sensible contrasted with your record capital. The vast majority of all, if an exchange never again bodes well, receive in return.

Surrendering to Greed

A few dealers feel that they have to press each and every pip out of a move in the market. There is cash to be made in the forex showcases consistently. Attempting to snatch each and every pip before a cash pair turns can make you hold positions excessively long and set you up to lose the gainful exchange that you are exchanging.

The arrangement appears glaringly evident here, simply don't be avaricious. It's fine to go for a sensible benefit yet there are a lot of pips to go around. Monetary forms keep on moving each day so there is no compelling reason to get that last pip; the following open door is directly around the bend.

Ambivalent Trading

Here and there you may wind up experiencing exchanging regret. This happens when an exchange that you open isn't promptly gainful and you start saying to yourself that you picked a misguided course. At that point you close your exchange and turn around it, just to see the market return the underlying way that you picked.

For this situation, you have to pick a bearing and stick with it. All that exchanging to and fro will simply make you constantly lose little bits of your record at once until your contributing capital is drained.

Attempting to Pick Tops or Bottoms

Numerous new merchants attempt to pick defining moments in cash sets. They will put an exchange on a couple, and as it props up off course, they keep on adding to their position being certain that it is going to pivot this time. If you exchange thusly, at last, you end up with significantly more presentation than you arranged, alongside a horrendously negative exchange.

It's ideal to exchange with the pattern. It's not worth the gloating rights to realize that you chose base accurately from 10 endeavors. If you think the pattern is going to change, and you need to take an exchange the new conceivable bearing, hang tight for an affirmation on the pattern change.

If you need to get a situation at the base, get the base in an upswing, not in a downtrend. If you need to open a situation at the top, pick a top when the market's creation a remedial move higher, not an upswing that is a piece of a bigger a downtrend.

Declining to Be Wrong

A few exchanges simply don't work out. It is human instinct to need to be correct, however in some cases you simply aren't. As a dealer, you simply need to acknowledge that you're off-base now and again and proceed onward, rather than sticking to being correct and winding up with a zero-balance exchanging account.

It is a troublesome activity, however now and again you simply need to concede that you committed an error. Possibly you entered the exchange for an inappropriate reasons, or it simply didn't work out the manner in which you arranged it. In any case, the best activity is simply concede the mix-up, dump the exchange, and proceed onward to the following chance.

Purchasing a System

There are some purported forex exchanging frameworks available to be purchased on the web. A few brokers are out there searching for the ever-tricky 100-percent precise forex exchanging framework. They continue purchasing frameworks and attempting them until at long last quitting any pretense of, choosing that there is no real way to win.

As another dealer, you should acknowledge that there is nothing of the sort as a free lunch. Succeeding at forex exchanging takes work simply like whatever else. You can discover accomplishment by structure your very own technique, methodology, and framework as opposed to purchasing useless frameworks on the web from not exactly trustworthy advertisers.

Most brokers have heard the measurements "95% of dealers lose cash" or "Just a couple of percent of merchants bring home the bacon at it."

While the numbers change somewhat from concentrate to examine, the truth of the matter is numerous merchants will lose cash and it can't be stayed away from. A wide range of reasons are given for the misfortunes, including poor cash the executives, terrible planning, or a poor technique. These elements do assume a job in individual exchanging achievement...

however there is a more profound motivation behind why a great many people lose.

Most dealers will lose paying little mind to what strategies they utilize. Regardless of whether all dealers knew how (remember, knowing and doing are two altogether different things) to exchange effectively dependent on current conditions, most brokers would in any case lose as time goes on. We should investigate why that is.

Value Extremes Require Nearly Everyone to Get Onboard

To comprehend why most dealers lose, we have to see how costs move. We additionally need to consider the enormous number of individuals who get included right when the cost is going to turn. This is the place the mass misfortunes occur.

At the point when a purchasing furor grabs hold in a market, it's difficult to recognize the truth about the development: something that will pass! Everything passes. However, at the time, individuals see other individuals purchasing, which makes them believe that they If they purchase now, at that point other individuals will purchase after them. Whenever you make a theoretical buy, you are doing so on the grounds that you accept other individuals will purchase after you, pushing the cost up which enables you to sell for a benefit.

Costs possibly rise if a greater number of individuals are stepping in to purchase than are eager to sell. While we can do a wide range of extravagant investigation and make gauges about value, all we are truly doing is making a wagered that individuals will step in to purchase or sell. We are breaking down individuals, since it is individuals that purchase and sell and cause costs to move. What's more, it's kin who cause rehashing designs, that we can exchange off of, in the monetary markets.

In this way, an upswing is made by an ever increasing number of individuals proceeding to drive the cost up. A cost can't go up some other way... individuals should be happy to pay ever more elevated costs. In the long run, there are no more individuals who are eager to purchase at more significant expenses, or there are a greater number of individuals ready to sell than purchase. The individuals who purchased close to the top are left holding the misfortunes.

One major issue is that countless individuals get included appropriate close to the top. For instance, a stock has been ascending for a long time and as more individuals get some answers concerning it they start heaping in. In any case, there is just a set number of individuals who care about that stock and are happy to get it. When the majority have heaped in, there is nobody else to purchase and the individuals who purchased before in the pattern begin to sell, which at that point terrifies the individuals who purchased late in the pattern, and the domino impact starts cutting costs down.

We should look a model: Bitcoin. Bitcoin had been rising consistently somewhere in the range of 2016 and 2017, yet with not a ton of enthusiasm from the overall population. Close to the center of 2017, significantly more individuals ended up intrigued. We can see this by what number of individuals Googled "bitcoin". We can accept that individuals looking for data on an item are not specialists, yet rather need to find out about it. The chart demonstrates that there was a blast in enthusiasm, bringing an entirely different group of purchasers into Bitcoin.

Maintaining a strategic distance from mass misfortunes, and making benefits as an individual, will be examined later on. For the time being, my point is to demonstrate that a great many people get included close to defining moments. Which means the vast majority lose, and are in the reality the impetus for turning the market the other way. There is a point of confinement to everything, and the mass free for all makes that utmost be hit.

En route up, there will be a lot of individuals who would prefer not to get included in light of the fact that they accept the cost is now excessively high. However, the market continues ticking higher thus a couple of the stragglers participate and purchase. Some still hold out and the market continues ticking higher. At last, 85% of the populace is bullish, and there are still a few stragglers… and the market props up. Individuals are broadcasting their accomplishments and reciting that blast and bust cycles are a relic of days gone by.

WHY YOU SHOULD START WITH SWING TRADING

Swing exchanging is a fruitful technique for stock exchanging that is regularly utilized by merchants who make a week by week or month to month living on their contributing. It is viewed as a close or medium term venture since it is an exchange that either represents the deciding moment itself more often than not in two to thirty days. It isn't the sort of exchange that long haul financial specialists would be keen on. Swing Trading endeavors to consolidate the best of two universes – the moderate pace of contributing and the fast potential increases of day exchanging.

So what is the meaning of swing exchanging? It is practiced through the examination of stock information. It tries to recognize a present stock or security that is ascending in value rapidly and hopes to do as such for a brief timeframe. A swing dealer buys the rising stock, rides the flood of expanding worth, and after that gets out before the market remedies and the value rapidly drops down. Furthermore, that is the stunt of swing exchanging; recognizing when to get in and afterward when to get out to create the best benefit.

FOCAL POINTS OF SWING TRADING

Restricted Focus

Swing exchanging is specialized in nature and dependent on after searching for exceptionally transient patterns where stocks increment in worth rapidly. As needs be, Swing exchanging time periods enable you to concentrate on the center market development and recognize pattern energy effectively. It just takes a few seconds to get your inclination on a swing exchanging time allotment. You don't need to get into a wide assortment of information territories, for example, organization asset reports and different things so as to get the required data to make an exchange. This increasingly tight spotlight encourages you focus on a couple of key territories that you will turn out to be generally excellent at. It's about simply the cost and patterns when swing exchanging. This reality likewise will in general make swing exchanging significantly less unpleasant than other transient exchanging styles, for example, Day Trading.

Know your Results rapidly

As was expressed, swing exchanging more often than not includes exchanges that are over with in only a couple of days as of recently. You will know how fruitful your technique has been periodically in under seven days. This enables you to have the option to continually change your swing exchanging procedure until you have it to the point where it is always procuring you cash.

Can Generate Monthly Income

Since you don't need to lounge around for quite a long time and years, for example, long haul contributing, you will know how a lot of cash you have made on your exchanges and the amount of that you can remove from your venture account as salary. You can augment the sum you acquire from doing as meager as three to five exchanges for each week that regularly are acknowledged and completed in under ten days.

Spares Time

It is the sort of exchanging that doesn't need to be continually observed so it is useful for speculators who don't have a great deal of time, for example, the individuals who exchange on low maintenance premise while holding down another all day work. When an individual has turned out to be capable at specialized investigation, again in accordance with the tight focal point of things you are taking a gander at about a stock, it doesn't set aside a ton of effort to distinguish the key patterns and make your exchanges.

Hazard Control

Maybe the most noteworthy bit of leeway of swing exchanging is its capacity to limit chance. Stop misfortunes are commonly littler than longer term exchanges. This takes into account you to put bigger estimated positions rather than very low utilized ones by means of the more extended term patterns. Another factor in the decrease of hazard is you are by and large making just three to five exchanges every week so you don't have this expansive range of speculations to mind; it enables you to keep extremely close track on your exchanges requiring just a short measure of time.

Swing exchanging can be a decent exchanging style for individuals who work during business sector hours yet at the same time need to be dynamic, generally transient brokers.

Assess the cost at which you need to enter an exchange and spot a purchase stop at that cost. If your exchange is filled, promptly place your defensive stop (some exchanging programming will enable you to put in various requests dependent on If/at that point situations, or you can do it physically).

Albeit medium-term hazard can be a detriment of swing exchanging, the holes that occasionally happen medium-term can likewise work in support of you If they hole toward your exchange. This enables you to make brisk, enormous, medium-term cash not accessible with day exchanging.

Swing exchanging enables you to set aside more effort to investigate the market you're exchanging and settle on exchanging choices an increasingly loosened up way without the time weight of day exchanging.

Focal points

Forex energy exchanging procedures are basically favorable in light of the fact that they are contained exchanging on wide market developments. While a solitary scalping exchange may just hope to bank a little benefit over a matter of only a couple of minutes, a swing exchange may occur more than 24 hours or more as the market remedies its estimating. This implies the potential increases from an effectively gauge swing exchange are immense, possibly into the high tens/many PIPs If you take care of business.

This additionally makes this kind of exchanging a proportionately modest approach to exchange. Since there are not many exchanges affected that are open over the more extended term, the exchanging expenses are insignificant and as an extent of the additions looked for, totally irrelevant, in this manner rendering the expense of the exchange a considerably less huge weight to shoulder.

Exchanging on the swing is additionally worthwhile from the perspective of the time speculation required. It is conceivable to accept your position and get with a momentary exchange before riding the wave as the value redresses, with no dynamic investment required other than watching out for execution. Especially If you've set your parameters for quits, swing exchanging is possibly time serious with regards to choosing which money pairings to exchange, as opposed to requiring a nearby, dynamic interest from the broker.

Advantages of Swing Trading

>> It isn't at all as tiring and worrying as the day exchanging seems to be; along these lines, there is no need of sitting before the PC screen the entire day. >> Here you can exploit the shortcomings of different dealers who are at the most the amateur and the tenderfoots in this type of exchanging.

>> There is really a constrained hazard for not getting to and holding up the stocks for a more drawn out timeframe.

>> The Institutional reserve chiefs are not ready to utilize the swing exchanging procedure in light of their significant level of holding up the elements.

WORKING ON THE FINANCIAL
MARKETS AND HOW TO AVOID IT

A money related market is a market where individuals exchange monetary protections and subordinates at low exchange costs. Protections incorporate stocks and securities, and valuable metals.

The expression "advertise" is now and again utilized for what are all the more carefully trades, associations that encourage the exchange monetary protections, e.g., a stock trade or item trade. This might be a physical area, (for example, the NYSE, LSE, JSE, BSE) or an electronic framework, (for example, NASDAQ). Much exchanging of stocks happens on a trade; still, corporate activities (merger, side project) are outside a trade, while any two organizations or individuals, for reasons unknown, may consent to offer stock from the one to the next without utilizing a trade.

Exchanging of monetary standards and bonds is to a great extent on a two-sided premise, albeit a few bonds exchange on a stock trade, and individuals are building electronic frameworks for these too, to stock trades.

The securities exchange, or values advertise as it is likewise known, is one of the world's most prominent and effectively exchanged money related markets. It's likewise a spot where numerous individuals go to attempt to profit, both rapidly and over the long haul. There are numerous approaches to profit in the securities exchange, utilizing both conventional procedures and some progressively imaginative techniques.

What Are Stocks?

Responsibility for in fact speaks to the proprietorship, or if nothing else incomplete possession, of organizations. Proprietors of stocks in many nations have a legitimate appropriate to cast a ballot at organization investors' gatherings and will get a notice when the gatherings are held. After offers are given by organizations, they can be (and typically are) exchanged progressively on the auxiliary market.

There are a few different ways to profit with the buy, possession and closeout of stock in the securities exchange:

Development Stocks

Stocks whose organizations are required to encounter solid development are known as development stocks.

One of the fundamental ways brokers can profit with them is holding their offers until they increment in cost, and after that offering them to take a benefit (also called a capital addition). Now and again, share costs will vacillate uncontrollably in unpredictable markets, offering merchants chances to purchase, sell and take benefits quickly.[1]

Initial public offering

At the point when organizations first issue offers to the general population, they hold introductory open contributions (IPOs) to permit first buy rights to potential purchasers. A few IPOs are intently viewed and intensely exchanged. That is on the grounds that stock costs from promising new organizations can be offered up rapidly from low levels to extremely elevated levels in a brief timeframe. This produces open doors for snappy and some of the time soak profits.[2]

Worth Stocks

As the name proposes, esteem stocks are those that are underestimated by the market, showing a decent can anticipate potential purchasers. Worth contributing can require careful examination of an organization's fiscal reports to comprehend its budgetary wellbeing and future potential, however this might merit the exertion.

Acclaimed financial specialist Warren Buffett is one understood defender of significant worth contributing. Roused by the worth contributing systems of contributing theoretician Benjamin Graham, Buffett had the option to store up a fortune searching out underestimated stocks over a time of quite a while. Graham accepted that stocks spoke to a decent arrangement when they were evaluated at 66% or less of their "inherent" value.

Pay Stocks

Holding salary stocks is a customary method to profit in the securities exchange. Loads of organizations that gain strong incomes frequently pay profits, as a rule on a quarterly premise, to investors. Stocks that pay generally higher profits, or salary stocks, can often profit for their proprietors. However, brokers may regularly need to amass a lot of such stocks to get noteworthy profit installments.

Stock Funds

Holding common assets, or trade exchanged assets, is another way that dealers can make cash on stocks. A reserve is comprised of a gathering of money related resources, regularly stocks, that are packaged all together security. Shared assets regularly require least buy sums and are not exchanged during business sector hours.

Trade exchanged assets are like common assets, yet are exchanged during business sector hours as though they were individual stocks and can be purchased and sold in littler augmentations than shared assets. Both common assets and trade exchanged finances that hold stocks frequently pay out profits from their property on a customary basis.

Investment opportunities And Futures

The alternatives and prospects markets are actually not part of the securities exchanges, however they can give great chances to profiting with stocks.

In choices exchanging, dealers can get the alternative to purchase or sell a stock at a predefined cost at a future lapse date. If the securities exchange's cost is higher or lower than the choice's predetermined strike cost at its lapse date, at that point the holder of the alternative can practice their purchasing or selling right and pocket the distinction between the two costs. Alternatives can likewise be purchased or sold on the optional market before the lapse date. Additionally, prospects agreements are sold for certain significant stock records and some individual stocks.

Prospects agreements are sold at an expected future cost for the record or stock. The agreements by and large lapse four times each year, once close to the finish of each quarter. If the stock or file worth is higher than the prospects cost at termination, the purchaser of the agreement can take a benefit. If the worth is lower, the merchant of the agreement takes a profit.

Favored Stock Vs. Basic Stock

Stocks are generally given in two kinds: favored stock and normal stock. Basic investors, as referenced above, are given democratic rights. Favored investors don't have casting a ballot rights. However, favored stock typically gets higher profit installments than normal stock and has more noteworthy assurances of reimbursement should the organization bow out of all financial obligations.

Some favored offers are likewise convertible into normal offers. These offers can be changed over at a predefined proportion. If the cost of the convertible favored offers is lower than the cost of basic offers after the transformation rate is applied, the favored offers can be traded for normal offers at a benefit to the shareholder.

Short-Selling

Short-selling a stock is another regular method for profiting with stocks. While brokers regularly consider purchasing, or going "long," on stocks they think will ascend in an incentive as a manner to pick up cash, short-selling adopts the contrary strategy.

Short venders get shares, as a rule from their dealer, so as to sell, or "short," stocks they think will fall in worth. After the offers fall in value, they repurchase them and return them to the loan specialist. They pocket the distinction in the cost at which they sold the offers and the lower cost at which they got them back.

Stock Splits

Stock parts can on occasion be affirmed by organization sheets and investors. At the point when a stock split happens, the investor is allowed a various number of extra offers for each offer held, in proportions of 2-to-1, 3-to at least 1. The estimation of each offer is partitioned in a comparing way. In any case, when a split happens, the investor's potential future property of the organization, and comparing riches, might be helped significantly.

Rundown

There are an assortment of approaches to profit in the securities exchange, and therefore it is where numerous dealers go to look for formation of riches. Stocks, similar to any money related exchanging, can include potential dangers and misfortunes. However, merchants may improve their odds by getting comfortable with the numerous roads wherein to utilize the financial exchange furthering their potential benefit.

Any feelings, news, inquire about, examinations, costs, other data, or connections to outsider locales are given as general market discourse and don't establish speculation guidance. FXCM won't acknowledge risk for any misfortune or harm including, without impediment, to any loss of benefit which may emerge legitimately or in a roundabout way from utilization of or dependence on such data.

CASH AND RISK MANAGEMENT
FOR SWING TRADING

As a swing merchant, your cash the executives procedure is the one variable that will give you the greatest edge in exchanging stocks. You can't control the business sectors however you can control your cash and your hazard on every single exchange that you make.

William O'neill, originator of Investors Business Daily, has said that, "The entire mystery to winning in the financial exchange is to lose the least sum conceivable when no doubt about it." I would concur with that!

Your cash the board procedure responds to these inquiries:

What amount of cash would it be advisable for me to chance on this exchange?

What number of offers would it be a good idea for me to purchase?

A decent exchanging framework or technique is completely useless without a strategy for dealing with your cash. You like to exchange stocks right? You like to profit in the business sectors right? All things considered, you won't have any cash to exchange with If you don't pursue great cash the board rehearses!

Your #1 objective as a swing dealer is to safeguard your capital with the goal that you can remain alive long enough to have some enormous victors that spread the expenses of your losing exchanges AND make a benefit. You achieve this through a sound cash the executives technique.

The 2% rule

Most brokers would concur that you ought not chance over 2% of your exchanging capital on a solitary exchange. The securities exchange is for the most part irregular. Nobody else is going to disclose to you this, however this is the truth of exchanging stocks.

So regardless of how great the diagram looks, quite possibly the stock won't go in your ideal heading and you will lose cash on the exchange. What amount of cash will you lose if this occurs?

On the first of every month, take a gander at the aggregate sum of cash in your exchanging account.

Suppose you have $30,000 dollars. Two percent of this sum is $600.00. That is the greatest sum you can lose on an exchange.

Position estimating

Presently suppose that you see a stock that has maneuvered into the TAZ and is currently exchanging at $25.00. It is seeming as though it will turn around so you conclude that you are going to exchange this stock. You initially need to make sense of where your stop will be. Try not to consider how a lot of cash you can make on an exchange, consider how a lot of cash you can lose if your wrong!

You establish that your stop will be at $24.00. So If you purchase the stock at 25.00 and your stop is at $24.00 then your hazard is $1.00 per share. Since you have just verified that the most you can chance on an exchange is $600.00 then you can purchase 600 portions of this stock.

This is in such a case that you get halted out you will lose $600.00, the most extreme sum you are permitted to lose. As a matter of fact the quantity of offers that you purchase ought to be somewhat less in light of the fact that you need to represent slippage and commissions.

By dealing with your cash accurately on each exchange you can unwind in such a case that you cause a misfortune it will be irrelevant to your record. This will likewise calm the passionate entanglements that plaque such huge numbers of merchants.

This is just one exchange! If you lose cash on this exchange, simply proceed onward to another. If you have a string of a few misfortunes in line either quit exchanging or lessen your position size to 1%.

Have a Risk Management Plan

Methodologies differ for swing exchanging, yet one thing effective swing dealers do is control hazard. So as to decide how a lot of capital you'll have to exchange, first build up the amount you're willing danger on each exchange (as far as stored capital) as this influences your positions size.

It's prescribed swing brokers chance under 2% of the record capital on single exchange. 1% or less is far better. If you store $10,000 into a record, that implies you can chance $100 (1% of $10,000) or $200 (2% of $10,000) per exchange. Pick which it will be and record it in your exchanging plan.

The above is your "account chance." It's the amount of your record you're willing to chance on each exchange. Next, there's "exchange hazard."

Exchange hazard is set utilizing a stop misfortune request it's a request that gets you out of a losing position at a particular cost. Your exchange hazard and the record hazard decide your position size. To perceive how this all fits together, how about we look a model from the securities exchange.

Position size = Account chance ($)/Trade Risk ($)

Expect you'll just hazard 1% of your capital per exchange, and have a $10,000 account; 1% of $10,000 is $100 (your "account chance"). If you'll likely be beginning with an alternate measure of capital, module an alternate record balance that is progressively reasonable to your circumstance.

All together keep our record hazard to 1% or less, each exchange ought to have a stop misfortune appended to it. If you purchase a stock at a $20, and put in a stop misfortune request at $19.50, your hazard on the exchange is $0.50 per share (your "exchange chance"). Since we can chance $100 (1% of the record) we can figure what number of offers we can take on the exchange:

Position size = $100/$0.50 = 200 offers.

200 offers is your position size, in this model. In view of record hazard and exchange chance, this is what number of offers you need to take for that particular exchange.

Seeing how position measuring functions is a key in deciding how a lot of capital you'll have to swing exchange stocks. Since you think about that, we can utilize it to perceive how a lot of your equalization/store ought to be If you need to swing exchange.

For direction on the best way to discover passage and stop misfortune levels, peruse the General Trading Strategies segment.

The amount Money You Need to Become a Stock Swing Trader

There's no base capital necessity to turn into a stock swing broker. Informal investor's (characterized as making multiple exchanges seven days that are opened and shut around the same time) are required to keep up a $25,000 balance in their record (in the US), however that is not a necessity for swing merchants. Simply ensure you don't wind up day exchanging a ton, else you'll be dependent upon this base.

The capital you require is subsequently identified with your position size, your record hazard and your exchange chance (as we saw over, these last three variables are connected).

You can likewise exchange on edge. Securities exchange swing merchants can have up to multiple times influence, which means If you store $10,000 you can buy up to $20,000 worth of stock. Record hazard is constantly founded on saved capital, not the influence sum!

Here are some essential rules to remember for swing exchanging stocks.

All exchanging is dangerous. Indeed, even with a stop misfortune on an exchange is conceivable to lose all your capital, or significantly more capital than you saved If you are exchanging on influence.

Hazard in any event $100 per exchange, generally commissions can be turned into an enormous obstacle to survive. If you chance $20 per exchange, for instance, commissions could add essentially to your misfortune, or genuinely disintegrate your benefit. On bigger sums, commissions become less of an issue.

Keep hazard to 1% or 2% of the record per exchange.

In view of these rules we can in a flash confirm that we need in any event $5,000 to $10,000 to much think about swing exchanging stocks. If we hazard 2% of our record per exchange (at any rate $100), at that point we need at any rate $5,000 (0.02 x $5,000 = $100). If we need to keep hazard lower, and hazard just 1% per exchange, at that point we need in any event $10,000 (0.01 x $10,000 = $100).

With these equalizations most stocks can be exchanged, even costly ones. For instance, expect you have a $5,000 record and see an incredible exchange to purchase a stock at $200. You feel good setting your stop misfortune at $190. This implies your exchange hazard is $10, and you are happy to hazard up to $100 on the exchange (account chance), which is 2% of $5,000. What number of offers would you be able to purchase? If you hazard $10 per share, you are permitted to purchase 10 offers (10 offers x $10 = $100 you are permitted to lose).

10 offers costs you 10 x $200 = $2,000. This is not exactly the capital you have in the record, so despite everything you have space to take more exchanges, particularly If you have influence (which is up to 2:1, giving you $10,000 in purchasing power on your $5,000 account).

Lower valued stocks work a similar way. Let's assume we discovered an exchange a $2 stock and were happy with putting our stop misfortune at $1.90. Our exchange hazard is $0.10, and we are happy to chance $100 (or more… as long as it is under 1% or 2% of our record balance). Fitting it into the position size equation: $100/$0.10 = 1000 offer position size. Indeed, this position just costs us $2000 ($2 x 1000 offers) so we have space for different exchanges the record.

So we can see that with $5,000, and being happy to hazard 2% per exchange (or with $10,000 and gambling 1% or 2%) we can swing exchange viably. Obviously increasingly capital can be used similarly. Similar ideas apply to a $100,000 account.

In the models over the stop misfortune is 5% away from the section ($10 chance on $200 stock, or $.10 on $2 stock), this is frequently satisfactory for swing exchanging, however the stop misfortune separation will clearly be influenced by your particular methodology. See Where to Place a Stop Loss for additional. The distance away the stop misfortune is will influence the position size.

As a fundamental standard guideline, you should begin swing exchanging stocks with in any event $5,000 to $10,000. If you fall beneath these equalizations, at that point you may wind up gambling a lot on each exchange, accepting we chance at any rate $100 per exchange (not as much as this, and commissions can turn into a colossal obstacle).

I prescribe gambling in any event $100 per exchange since we should just take exchanges where we hope to take more If we win that we will lose if the exchange turns sour. For instance, If I chance $100, I am ordinarily hoping to make in any event $200, $300, or more, on my triumphant exchanges. However, If I just gambled $10, I may just make $20 or $30, and the majority of that would be eaten up by commissions... not great. So If you need to profit, you have to put a better than average measure of cash on hold. As the record develops, you will chance more, and subsequently ideally make more.

If you hope to make 5% every month (the amount you cause will to change by procedure) on a $30,000 account, that is a $1500 every month salary, less commissions. If you attempt to swing exchange with $1000 or $2500 (and make 5% every month), the vast majority of the $50 to $125 benefit

Risk from 1% to 2% of your account balance, which means a $ 100,000 account that could risk up to $ 1,000 to $ 2,000 per transaction (and hopefully do much more to offset), instead a $ 100 risk level with a minimum account balance.

SPECIALIZED ANALYSIS FOR
SWING TRADING

Most financial specialists will purchase their positions and after that clutch them, hanging tight for economic situations to improve before they make an exchange. Along these lines, they can profit by a decent return. There are those financial specialists who are fantastically quiet, sitting tight for quite a long time and gathering little profits after some time as their profits. At that point there are those that are in a rush to get their profits, particularly if there is a little thankfulness in the pair they are exchanging. That is the thing that swing exchanging is about. To benefit as much as possible from this procedure, you have to realize these three swing exchanging pointers.

1. Moving Average

The first is the moving normal where the emphasis is on distinguishing a pattern as well as affirming the pattern. The most straightforward moving normal pointer to utilize is the basic moving normal. It necessitates that all the shutting costs be included down for a particular number of days, and after that taking the aggregate and partitioning it by a similar number. On a chart, it is conceivable to plot the normal so one can comprehend what's going on with the market cost.

2. Relative Strength Index

To decide the best positions in the forex advertise for swing exchanging, you additionally look over the second pointer which is among the best specialized markers for swing exchanging. This is the RSI which represents Relative Strength Index. This pointer gives data that is perfect to passage into the market. It assists with the examination of short flag, under a specific assumption. That is the reality the market might be overbought or might be oversold. It is an incredible procedure when the market has demonstrated to be level just as range bound.

3. Visual Analysis Indicator

Specialized pointers give an abundance of data, yet once in a while, it is a lot simpler to have a visual example to work with. This makes it a lot simpler to perceive what's going on inside the market and guide your choice. This is the third swing exchanging marker, visual investigation. There are a few examples that one can pay special mind to particularly as a marker for a swing exchanging system.

Tips to Make You a Better Swing Trader

Since you know the best swing exchange markers, here are a few hints that will make you an astounding swing merchant. Start off by recognizing your help just as opposition levels utilizing specialized examination. This implies you ought to have the option to peruse the diagram to decide the zone inside the graph where there is some help or opposition.

Figure out how to recognize wide range candles as these make it simpler to uncover defining moments inside the swing exchange. With this, you will have the option to discover when a stock may switch.

Swing exchanging is the key to progress for some brokers. Investigate it, study how it is done, and make fast profits for unexpected changes in the market.

Candles and Oscillators for Successful Swing Trades

Candles and oscillators can be utilized freely, or in mix, to feature potential transient exchanging openings. Swing dealers have practical experience in utilizing specialized investigation to exploit transient value moves. Effectively exchanging these swings requires the capacity to precisely decide both pattern heading and pattern quality. This should be possible using diagram designs, oscillators, volume examination, fractals, and an assortment of different strategies. This article will concentrate on utilizing oscillators and candle examples to recognize swing exchanges.

Pinpointing a Reversal

Swing dealers can search for transient inversions in the cost to catch inevitable value moves toward that path. The initial step is to locate the correct conditions for an inversion, which should be possible with either candles or oscillators. Candle inversions are described by uncertainty candles or candles that demonstrate a solid move in assumption (from purchasing to selling or offering to purchasing), while oscillator feature potential inversions by means of uniqueness.

Oscillator Divergence

Dissimilarity is the point at which the cost is moving the other way of a force oscillator. Consider it in material science terms: If you hurl a ball noticeable all around, it loses force before it inverts course. This is likewise how inversions can happen in the financial exchange. Force eases back before stock costs invert. Uniqueness may indicate when the force is easing back and a potential inversion is approaching. Not all value inversions are conjecture by difference, however many are.

Difference is a decent beginning stage for an exchange. Dissimilarity doesn't generally need to display, however If uniqueness is available, the candle designs (talked about straightaway) are probably going to be all the more dominant and liable to bring about better exchanges.

The accompanying outline indicates disparity. The cost was moving higher however the oscillator—the relative quality record (RSI), for this situation—was moving lower. The uniqueness indicated shortcoming in the ascent, which was likewise noticeable by taking a gander at the value activity as the cost could scarcely make new highers before falling once more. At last the value wound up falling essentially.

SWING TRADING STRATEGIES FOR BEGINNERS AND FOR ADVANCED

In this segment, you will gain proficiency with my total swing exchanging methodology - from start to finish! To begin with, read this page to get an outline of how the technique functions:

Purchasing shortcoming and selling quality is the specialty of purchasing pullbacks. Stocks that are in up patterns will draw back offering an okay purchasing chance and stocks that are in down patterns will mobilize offering a generally safe shorting opportunity.

As a swing broker, you need to trust that these open doors will happen in light of the fact that...

Doesn't it bode well to purchase a stock after a flood of selling has happened as opposed to getting trapped in an auction?

Doesn't it bode well to short a stock after a flood of purchasing has happened as opposed to getting trapped in a convention?

Totally! If you are purchasing a stock, at that point you need the same number of dealers out of the stock before you get in. Then again, If you are shorting a stock, at that point you need the same number of purchasers in the stock before you get in. This gives you an okay section that you can oversee successfully.

Purchasing pullbacks and shorting rallies

Where do you purchase a pullback and where do you short a meeting? You get them and short them in the Traders Action Zone (TAZ). Here is and model on the long side:

The main pullback

These are actually what the name suggests. It is the first after an adjustment in pattern. How would you recognize an adjustment in pattern - when the 10 SMA crosses the 30 EMA. After that occurs, you search for a passage when the stock gets into the TAZ

This is the most solid sort of section into a stock and this is the possible region where institutional cash is going to come into the stock. If you just exchange one example, this ought to be it! You can get into a stock toward the start of a pattern, at a point of okay, and you can take halfway benefits and ride the pattern to finishing! What more might you be able to request?

Goodness better believe it, talking about getting in on the start of a pattern. This next arrangement fits conveniently into an Elliott wave design...

First pullback after a breakout

There is one other sort of pullback worth referencing and that is the principal pullback after a breakout.

If you are taking a gander at a stock that is exchanging sideways or shaping a basing example, and it abruptly breaks out of the example, you can hope to purchase the main pullback after the breakout. This likewise gives you an okay section into a stock that will probably proceed with the present pattern.

What criteria do you use to purchase a stock? I figured you could never inquire! We purchase stocks after a flood of selling has happened. This bodes well right? If you purchase a stock and, at that point out of the blue it begins to fall you will be caught with a misfortune. Ouch! In this way, we trust that the stock will fall first. This is designated "purchasing force backs". Also, we purchase these draw moves in the Traders Action Zone (TAZ for short).

Swing Trading Strategies - Two Tips For Anyone Looking to Try Out Swing Trading

Swing is the most perfectly awesome exchanging technique or style with regards to money exchanging or some other sort of market. Merchants have a wide range of techniques accessible to exchange markets with however none verge on offering a similar sort of high rewards with insignificant hazard that swing exchanging does. This doesn't imply that swing exchanging is an idiot proof style of exchanging, yet what it means is that a merchant is giving themselves the most flawlessly awesome chances of pulling the trigger on a triumphant exchange each time an exchange is put. If you might want to take a stab at swing exchanging, at that point there are two significant elements that must consider before choosing which market to exchange and how to swing exchange it.

The primary thing any swing dealer must do is guarantee that the market or instrument they need to public exhibitions a higher inclination to drift than not slant. I'm not catching this' meaning precisely? Since this style of exchanging removes lumps from market swings, the best markets to use with this style are ones that pattern in substantially more normal and smooth ways. Not all business sectors act a similar way and you will locate that some appear to never pattern and others are excessively flighty and bounce around everywhere.

The least demanding approach to check if an instrument patterns well or not is to open up a four hour to every day diagram and investigate the previous a while of value activity. If you notice value going all over in an apparently liquid way with unmistakable swings in value activity, at that point there is a decent possibility that you could swing exchange this market. If you see that value erratically bounces around or goes sideways with no obvious market swings, at that point you'd be best off skirting this market and searching for a progressively reasonable one.

The last factor is that of exchanging with the pattern. Swing merchants are pattern devotees by their very nature and this is something that numerous new dealers are not happy with. One of the principle purposes behind completing the past pattern keep an eye on the instrument you need to exchange is on the grounds that not exclusively does swing exchanging expect cost to causes swings to here and there however dealers of this exchanging style are for the most part considered pattern supporters. You remain to make considerably more over the long haul by going with the pattern and not against it. It sounds basic and it is something that all dealers know about yet you might be astonished at exactly what number of can't keep this basic standard.

Most brokers are going to purchase breakouts. The word breakouts sounds so energizing isn't that right?

The issue with purchasing breakouts is that it is not really every generally safe. Consider it. If you are purchasing stocks when every other person is, at that point why should left purchase the stock after you get in?

Additionally think about this: most of breakouts fall flat and return (pullback) to the breakout point!

Building Your Swing Trading Prowess

Remaining large and in charge implies you can learn constantly or developing yourself. Unfortunately, you can't just turn into a swing trading specialist and execute your trades with nary a solitary issue. Hell, a master military craftsman doesn't stop in the wake of gaining their dark belt — for what reason would a swing trader?

The accompanying activity things will assist you with remaining solid all through your swing trading vocation:

Admit to misfortunes when they happen. Markets have a method for lowering even the most talented traders in the event that they let their self images impede their trading. A few traders clutch losing positions in the expectations that they can in the long run break even — an arrangement that obliterates a record over the long haul. A losing position not exclusively may lose more money however it additionally ties up capital that could be put resources into all the more encouraging trading openings.

Be an understudy of the markets. Effective swing traders absorb constantly data. The markets are continually changing, with new investment vehicles showing up and new laws being presented. As a swing trader, you should keep up scholarly interest. Reading books is one approach to consistently remain educated. Check out understanding your positions and reading the ace and con contentions on them.

Attempt to protect yourself however much as could reasonably be expected from others' feelings, regardless of whether the individual is an Average Joe or a Wall Street investigator. Keep in mind, Wall Street is a network, and experts convey their assessment reports to hundreds, if not thousands, of traders and portfolio administrators. Reading those reports can lead you to think like the investigator does — and like hundreds of others do. Great execution doesn't drop by duplicating what every other person is doing.

Don't visit message boards . Message boards regularly cultivate a gathering attitude that a position ought to carry on a specific way. You don't have any desire to assemble knowledge from only anybody on the

Internet. Or maybe, stick to confided in sources and structure your very own feeling on issues.

CANDLESTICK ANALYSIS AND CHART PATTERNS FOR SWING TRADING

Candle diagrams are a specialized apparatus that pack information for various time periods into single value bars. This makes them more helpful than conventional open-high, low-close bars (OHLC) or basic lines that draw an obvious conclusion of shutting costs. Candles fabricate designs that anticipate value heading once finished. Appropriate shading coding adds profundity to this brilliant specialized apparatus, which goes back to eighteenth century Japanese rice brokers.

Steve Nison brought candle examples toward the Western world in his prevalent 1991 book, "Japanese Candlestick Charting Techniques." Many dealers would now be able to recognize many these arrangements, which have bright names like bearish foreboding shadow spread, evening star and three dark crows. Furthermore, single bar examples including the doji and sledge have been joined into many long-and short-side exchanging systems.

Candle Pattern Reliability

Not all candle examples work similarly well. Their enormous prevalence has brought down unwavering quality since they've been deconstructed by mutual funds and their calculations. These well-financed players depend on lightning-speed execution to exchange against retail speculators and conventional reserve chiefs who execute specialized investigation systems found in famous writings. At the end of the day, fence stock investments directors use programming to trap members searching for high-chances bullish or bearish results. However, solid examples keep on showing up, considering short-and long haul benefit openings.

Here are five candle designs that perform incredibly well as antecedents of value course and energy. Every work inside the setting of encompassing value bars in foreseeing higher or lower costs. They are likewise time delicate in two different ways. To begin with, they just work inside the confinements of the graph being surveyed, regardless of whether intraday, every day, week by week or month to month. Second, their intensity diminishes quickly three to five bars after the example has finished.

Top 5 Candlestick Patterns

This analysis is based on the work of Thomas Bulkowski, who, in his 2008 book "The Candlestick Card Encyclopedia", determined the performance ratings for candle samples. Provides statistics for two types of expected results: investing and continuing. Candle inversion models predict a change in price direction, while continuation models predict an extension in the current price direction.

In the following examples, a white candle indicates a closing footprint larger than the opening opening, while a black candle indicates a closing footprint smaller than the opening opening.

Three lines strike

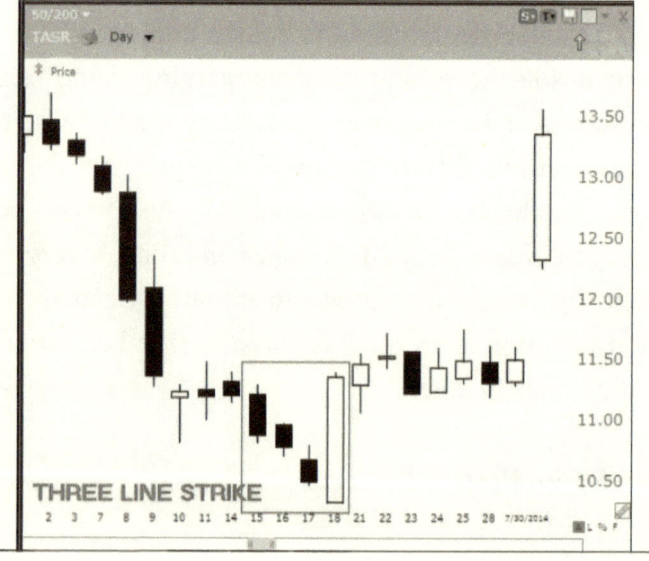

An upside down three-line pattern cuts three black candles in a falling trend. Each lane is lowered and closed near the intrabar depression. The fourth lane opens farther down but invests in a wide range beyond the bar that closes above the top of the first candle in a row. The opening footprint also marks the bottom of the fourth lane. According to Bulkowski, this turnaround predicts higher prices with an accuracy of 84%.

Two black Gapping

The pattern of the continuation of the two bearish black holes appears after a noticeable peak of the upward trend, with a downward deviation yielded by two black bars showing lower ones below. This pattern predicts that the decline will continue to decline further, triggering a larger downward trend. According to Bulkowski, this model predicts lower prices with an accuracy of 68%.

Three black crows

The bearish three dark crows inversion pattern begins at or close to the high of an uptrend, with three dark bars posting lower lows that nearby close intrabar lows. This pattern predicts that the decline will continue to try and lower lows, maybe triggering a broader-scale downtrend. The most bearish rendition begins at another high (point An on the chart) since it traps buyers entering energy plays. As indicated by Bulkowski, this pattern predicts lower prices with a 78% precision rate.

Night Star

The bearish night star inversion pattern begins with a tall white bar that conveys an uptrend to another high. The market holes higher on the following bar, however crisp buyers neglect to show up, yielding a thin range candle. A hole down on the third bar completes the pattern, which predicts that the decline will continue to try and lower lows, maybe triggering a broader-scale downtrend. As indicated by Bulkowski, this pattern predicts lower prices with a 72% precision rate.

Surrendered Baby

The bullish surrendered child inversion pattern shows up at the low of a downtrend, after a progression of dark candles print lower lows. The market holes lower on the following bar, however crisp dealers neglect to show up, yielding a limited range doji candle with opening and closing prints at a similar price. A bullish hole on the third bar completes the pattern, which predicts that the recuperation will continue to much higher highs, maybe triggering a broader-scale uptrend. As indicated by Bulkowski, this pattern predicts higher prices with a 70% exactness rate.

The Bottom Line

Candle patterns catch the consideration of market players, yet numerous inversion and continuation signals radiated by these patterns don't work dependably in the cutting edge electronic condition. Luckily, insights by Thomas Bulkowski show unordinary precision for a thin choice of these patterns, offering traders actionable buy and sell signals.

Chart Patterns For Swing Traders

Profitable Chart Patterns For Swing Traders

Here are four profitable chart patterns that you can utilize whenever you are searching for sections into individual stocks. Wait! There is no sacred goal. These patterns can and will come up short. You should manage your cash effectively!

The four chart patterns are:

- T-30
- Ghost Town
- Swing Trap (my personal top choice)
- Side Trap

Read increasingly about these patterns beneath..

T-30 chart pattern

This is the one chart pattern that I trade the frequently. If you are new to trading stocks, at that point start with this pattern! It is easy to distinguish, easy to learn, and easy to trade. What more might you be able to request?

How to Trade the T-30 Chart Pattern

The setup

The name T-30 refers to a "tail" that slices down through the "30" period exponential moving average. This looks like a hammer candlestick pattern on the chart but it doesn't have to be a perfect hammer to be considered a T-30. Also, the color of the real body is not important. This tail on the chart flushes other traders out of the stock.

Note: There is nothing special about the 30 period moving average. It is just a reference. Look to the left on the chart to determine support and resistance.

When you are trading any kind of tail or hammer pattern, always look for volume to be higher than the previous day. This suggests that many traders were shaken out and demand is picking up. This is important!

How to trade this pattern

There a numerous approaches to trade this setup depending on your ideal hazard/reward. I'll disclose to you how I trade it and give you an elective that you might need to consider.

The passage

If you can trade during the day, at that point buy the stock on the day of the hammer (tail) close to the end of the day. You not require any sort of "confirmation" or whatever else. You just need to see that this stock is at a support level and that request is coming into the stock (volume). That is all the confirmation that you need.

If you can't trade during the day, at that point place your buy stop over the high of this hammer day. The following day you should verify whether you get filled and afterward place your stop loss order. You could likewise utilize a section order.

The stop loss order

There are two alternatives for the placement of your stop loss order. Every ha advantages and disadvantages. You choose what is directly for you.

Choice 1:

Put your stop under the low of the hammer. The advantage to this is your stop is far away from your entrance price and you won't almost certainly get stopped out rashly. The disadvantage to this is on the grounds that your stop is so far away, you should buy less offers so as to agree to your cash management rules.

Alternative 2:

Move down to the hour long chart and put your stop under a support zone closer close to the real body of the candle. The advantage to this is you find a good pace shares in light of the fact that your stop is closer to your buy price. The disadvantage to this is on the grounds that your stop is so close, you may get stopped out more frequently, before a major move happens.

Personally, I lean toward choice 1. I have no issue buying less offers so as to have an effective trade. I like that fact that my stop is far away from the "market clamor". At that point I can kick back and wait persistently for the stock to move in my favor.

Taking profits

At the point when you are trading wide range days like hammers, you will find out that multiple occasions, the stock will trade sideways for a day or two. That is fine. You are already in the stock simply waiting for other traders to enter. Likewise, the days that follow a hammer are normally low instability, slender range days like stars or doji's.

Show restraint! Try not to get on edge to move your stop up. Wait for the stock to really move in your favor before you start trailing your stop.

When the stock moves in your favor, at that point you securely start to trail your stop utilizing your favorite exit strategy to secure profits.

Trading tips

Concentrate on those stocks where the real body of the candle is close to the 30 EMA. You need however many traders as could be allowed shaken out of this stock before you get in.

This setup is turned around for short situations aside from now you are searching for stocks with a falling star pattern through a declining 30 EMA.

Give more weight to setups with numerous tails more than a few days.

Give more weight to setups where the stock holes from the past candle to end the day in hammer.

Continuously look to one side on the chart to make sure the stock is at a huge support or resistance territory.

At the point when great chart patterns turn sour

Indeed, you will have losing trades with this pattern. There is no pattern that will ensure every single winning trade! However, with appropriate cash, trade, and self management, you can do very well with this setup.

THE ART OF TECHNICAL THEORY

Technical analysis is the craft of reading a security price chart with volume and deciding the security's presumable heading leveraging the strength of buyers and sellers. Technical analysis can go from the straightforward (deciphering a chart pattern) to the mind boggling (performing intermarket analysis and deciphering markers dependent on differential conditions). Essential chart translation is a significant ability, yet swing traders ordinarily depend on pointers and intermarket analysis.

The technical expert is essentially worried about the accompanying inquiries:

Is this security in a bull or bear market in the short and long haul?

Is the security drifting or in a trading range?

Who's in charge of the market — buyers or sellers?

Is the strength of the buyers/sellers expanding or melting away?

What price point shows an inversion or disappointment?

What signals the time to enter?

What signals the time to exit?

Seeing how and why technical analysis works

So for what reason does technical analysis work? In what manner can looking at past price history perhaps give knowledge into future price developments?

Market participants, acting alone, respond comparatively to significant news. Technical analysis is partly founded on the brain research of groups. Despite the fact that all investors may not be congregated in a solitary room, they're all human. Consequently, they're helpless to similar emotions all people share: covetousness, dread, trust, and so forth. Security prices would be exceptionally hard to break down if everybody trading were Spock-like — splendidly sensible without any emotions disrupting the general flow.

Market players have memories. Traders, investors and other market players have references about their purchases or sales of securities. The price they pay when buying value affects the likelihood of a sale (although there should be a slight difference in that choice). They recall their price tag and, normally, need to either make a profit or break even. If the security price swoons after they buy shares, they're probably going to feel torment. Also, if the price recuperates to their unique price tag, many will be glad to sell to break even. What these traders and investors frequently don't realize is that hundreds, if not thousands, of others are encountering these equivalent emotions. This reality is the reason certain price levels are more noteworthy than others. Securities will in general discover support (a level at which security prices quit falling and begin to rise) and opposition (a level at which security prices quit rising and begin to fall) at round numbers.

I'm astonished at how regularly traders place buy limit or sell limit orders at round price figures. Don't they realize that numerous different traders might be doing precisely the same thing, and that their activities may prevent the price from consistently arriving at that level? Simply, a sell limit of $100 isn't excessively splendid, in light of the fact that different traders or investors likely put orders at that equivalent round number. What's more, their orders may prevent yours from ever get-ting executed (the staggering stockpile of shares at that level will drive the stock to withdraw before coming to $100). Then again, a sell limit of $98.71 is smart, since it's impossible that different traders put in a request at that particular price, and you have a greatly improved possibility of your order getting executed.

Smart investors' activities appear on the chart. Smart money regularly refers to investment money made by institutional investors who buy or sell securities dependent on sound, contemplated analysis. These investors have the assets to call the providers and clients of firms they put resources into and can determine with a high level of certainty whether a company's profit are on-or off-track. Smart money likewise comprises insiders at a firm who have a data advantage over other market participants and may trade on that data.

Dumb money, then again, refers to investment money made by beginners who buy or sell securities for the rush of investment. Dumb money can incorporate retirement plans or corporate plans that strip securities that never again meet the plans' criteria. This selling pressure pushes prices down without any justifiable cause. Dumb money can likewise incorporate institutional investors who buy or sell stocks since they fall in affection with their investments. In all honesty, institutional investors are dependent upon similar impulses and enthusiastic swings experienced by all traders.

People with knowledge of a company's possibilities can just exploit that knowledge by trading on the open market. Their trading appears on the ticker tape (it's the law). So in the event that you realize that Microsoft will have a blowout quarter (by lawful methods, obviously, and not through insider knowledge), you can't profit from that knowledge with the exception of by buying shares. Furthermore, your buying is going to appear as volume on a price chart. Other people who may not think about the blowout quarter can, regardless, surmise that something is up when they see Microsoft's shares ascending on substantial volume.

Evaluating the technical points of interest and detriments

Since the price chart shows all accessible open and private data, technical analysis can truly sparkle brilliant when prices separate from their fundamentals. Opportunity is most noteworthy when you're in the minority, however right. If everybody, including you, expects shares of Coca-Cola to progress nicely, you won't make a lot of cash since every other person has just arrived at a similar resolution as you. However, in the event that you think something is appallingly off-base at a company and every other person is on the opposite side, you remain to make a huge profit in case you're correct and the group needs to address its aggregate supposition by selling stock.

For instance, shares of Enron were tumbling in late 2000 notwithstanding what gave off an impression of being excellent fundamentals. Price drops were met by updates and buy suggestions by Wall Street examiners who, utilizing all accessible open information, determined that shares spoke to a significant worth.

However, prices continued falling. A swing trader utilizing technical analysis would presume that something wasn't right. In the case of everything was peachy, why were shares falling? Something must be up. Also, sufficiently sure, something was up — something naughty to be sure. Investors utilizing fundamental analysis, then again, are frequently cautioned of basic breaks in a company's monetary situation after it's past the point of no return.

Despite the advantage of leeway technical analysis has of flagging data that you may not know, this system isn't a fix just for your trading burdens. Reading a chart includes a level of translation, and sometimes whipsaws or signs can give you one sign, just to switch a short while later. Additionally, a significant occasion can happen that nobody thinks about. Therefore, you'll never know with assurance that a particular chart pattern or pointer will yield a profitable sign. Swing traders (for sure, all traders) need to figure out how to live with this vulnerability, which additionally exists in fundamental analysis (or any analysis method, so far as that is concerned). Some swing traders are in reality wrong most of the time, yet at the same time very effective. Why? Since the numerous washouts are little, though the couple of victors are gigantic.

The two principle segments of technical analysis

This book covers the two significant parts of technical analysis: charting and utilizing technical indicators. Reading charts and utilizing indicators are of equivalent significance to the swing trader who utilizes technical analysis, so you ought to be proficient at both. (Remember that technical indicators are to a great extent unhelpful If you don't comprehend fundamental chart pattern understanding.)

Reading charts

Charting is the analysis of securities dependent on patterns, which security prices follow, just as volume. The intrigue of stock charts for some is their usability. Indeed, even fundamentals-based investors who don't trust in or utilize technical analysis raise a stock chart before buying another position just to see where the security has been as of late. Supervisors with no foundation in charting at all still use it somewhat. As a swing trader, you can utilize many chart types, including line charts, bar charts, and candlestick charts.

In this book, I break the discourse of patterns in two:

Mainstream chart patterns: The patterns you'll discover generally valuable in your swing trading, similar to head-and-shoulders and cup-and-handle arrangements, may show up whether you're utilizing a line, bar, or candlestick chart.

Candlestick-explicit chart patterns: These chart patterns, such as morning and night stars and bearish overwhelming patterns, are effectively distinguished when utilizing candlestick charts

Utilizing technical indicators

A technical indicator resembles a compass: It helps steer you in the correct direction. The demonstration of utilizing technical indicators, which I spread in Chapter 5, is a two-advance procedure:

1. Apply technical indicators to security prices.

Technical indicators are scientific recipes that, when applied to security prices, plainly streak either buy or sell signals. They to a great extent expel subjectivity from the analysis of chart patterns. Technical indicators principally fall into two classifications: trending and non-trending.

- Trending indicators are intended to search for noteworthy alters in course and enable you to ride through clamor (immaterial changes in security prices) that may occur throughout a couple of days. They measure the strength of these patterns and sign inversions, so you ought to apply trending indicators to securities that are reliably rising or falling.

- Non-trending indicators measure the strength of buyers and sellers where alters in course happen every now and again. They frequently institutionalize late price history — state, by setting up the high and low prices during the period — and measure the security's relative situation inside that institutionalized range. Non-trending indicators additionally create overbought and oversold signals. Overbought just methods the security has ascended excessively high and is due for a course revision, and oversold implies the security has fallen excessively low and is due for an inversion. You ought to apply non-trending indicators to securities that sway between two price levels, when the market participants to a great extent concur on the security's worth and the swings between the two price boundaries.

Not all indicators reveal to you whether a security is in trending mode or non-trending mode, however depending on the ones that do is helpful. Not all indicators are proper at a solitary point in time. Technical indicators are dependent upon client inputs. These inquiries partly clarify why no indicator is continually going to give the right sign. Many swing traders search out the Holy Grail indicator or framework that yields the right signals inevitably, yet no such indicator exists. You should depend on your comprehension of the security being referred to and apply indicators prudently.

2. Analyze the strength of the security comparative with the general market.

Relative strength analysis includes contrasting the exhibition of a security with a general market or industry by searching for divergences between the price of the security and the general market, which you can see in the wake of applying technical indicators. A dissimilarity happens when a security's price moves to new highs or new lows, and the technical indicator doesn't affirm that strength or shortcoming. The indicator is flagging that the security price isn't recounting to the entire story. Divergences are incredible signals since they convey data in opposition to the apparent pattern.

Fundamental Theory

In the event that you begin to perspire when you hear the expression fundamental analysis and get on edge when you consider all the extreme work that goes into dissecting a company, don't stress. I follow the K.I.S.S. (Keep It Simple, Stupid) approach with regards to fundamental analysis.

The material on fundamental analysis that I present in this book won't set you up for your MBA. Or maybe, it will control you through the key parts of a firm's fundamentals that have the greatest effect on share prices.

The fundamental expert is constantly posing the accompanying inquiries:

What is this present company's worth comparative with its friends?

What is this current company's development rate?

What are this current company's returns on capital and obligation levels?

At the point when you discover the responses to these questions, you begin to get a thought of what price the company's shares ought to reasonably trade at. You're not going to land at the intrinsic qualities that Wall Street examiners slave over ascertaining (intrinsic worth refers to the genuine estimation of a company and is recognized from market esteem, which is the worth the market is right now doling out to the firm). In any case, you don't have to know the estimation of the shares you trade down to the penny. If shares are valued at $15, and you realize shares ought to be somewhere in the range of $25 and $32, do you truly need to burn through many hours ascertaining the careful figure? Not a chance.

Understanding how and why fundamental analysis works

Understanding how fundamental analysis works is somewhat simpler than under-standing how technical analysis works. Here's the reason this procedure is viable:

The higher the earnings of a company, the more others will pay for a bit of that company. If you claim a condo that produces $1,000 in income every month, what amount would you esteem that cash stream? Various individuals would esteem the condo in an unexpected way, contingent upon their hazard resistance levels and the sureness of that cash stream proceeding. However, clearly, if the condo were delivering income of $2,000 every month, it would be worth twofold what it was worth when it was creating $1,000 every month.

Fundamental analysis isn't that unique, then again, actually as opposed to delivering rental income of $1,000 every month, organizations produce earnings and report them quarterly. Obviously, investors don't ordinarily get a firm's whole income since quite a bit of it is reinvested in the business. In any case, the fact of the matter is, fundamental analysis works since it measures a company's worth dependent on its normal future earnings.

Arbitrageurs hold prices under wraps. Another significant reason fundamental analysis works is that arbitrageurs are searching for riskless profits. For instance, assume a security is trading at $25 per share, and the company is valued at $1 billion. In the event that the firm had $2 billion in cash on its books and no obligation, an arbitrageur would step in to exploit the mispricing. The arbitrageur could buy the company for $1 billion and afterward pay for the purchase utilizing the cash the company has on its books. So fundamental analysis works since firms, governments, and people are constantly searching for riskless profits.

OK, you're persuaded that fundamental analysis has merit, however would you be able to profit by it in your swing trading? The appropriate response is yes. In any case, you ought to know about its limitations and how you can address them:

In contrast to technical analysis, you can't consistently apply fundamental analysis to securities. A swing trader who sees how to decipher chart patterns and technical indicators experiences a similar procedure whether the individual in question is trading corn, cotton, gold, oil, stocks, trade traded funds, or common funds. The chart analysis is the equivalent, and opposition and bolster both apply in light of the fact that market participants carry on in comparable manners paying little heed to what they're trading.

Master the fundamental analysis of cotton, be that as it may, and you aren't greatly improved off when you come to trading oil. Master the fundamental analysis of telecom shares, and you'll confront another ballgame with regards to banks. Contrasts continue between market fundamentals and how you examine them. Consequently, swing traders who depend on fundamental analysis regularly should represent considerable authority in a couple of markets.

Fundamentals change less regularly than chart prices. A company reports its earnings and marketing projections once at regular intervals. Swing trading dependent on a report that is two months old can be risky in light of the fact that whatever worth the report contained was likely joined in the company's price during the initial hardly any days after the report was discharged. This reality doesn't mean you ought to disregard updates on a company that isn't later. Yet, it means that you don't have any desire to buy a security dependent on a news report gave two months prior that business are seething. The reason for the purchase must be an ongoing impetus or the combination of good technicals (a chart) and great fundamentals.

Studying the fundamental favorable advantages and drawbacks

Fundamental analysis has its pluses and minuses. A few aspects, for example, its accentuation on industry elements and rivalry, make it appropriate for the swing trader; different aspects, for example, its focus on esteem acknowledgment over the long haul, make it a poor swing trading apparatus.

The upsides of fundamentals are fixated on the focus on esteem — what a firm is really worth. Fundamental analysis

- Appraisals a firm's intrinsic worth paying little mind to where the market trades
- Fuses industry and market impacts, which can drive security prices couple
- Prevails upon the long haul — fundamentals drive the prices of securities Assumes the market isn't right on occasion

Obviously, fundamental analysis additionally has its shortcomings since it

- Can be incorrect in the short term when you most need it
- Is more abstract than technical analysis
- Depends vigorously on your ability to decipher applicable market data

- Doesn't give reference focuses on ways out should your suspicions be incorrect

SWING TRADING WITH TOOLS
AND INDICATORS

This is a brisk outline of three of the best exchanging pointers for day and swing merchants the same. If you are another broker, at that point it is significant for you to comprehend that no pointer or oscillator is going to make you exchange gainfully quickly, so don't go on a totally pointless pursuit to discover one that will. Become familiar with a chosen few markers and the techniques and procedures to utilize them adequately. Ace them, and afterward find out additional.

If you somehow happened to take a swing exchanging course at this moment, I accept that the present economic situations would permit any merchant utilizing the best possible exchanging method to accomplish strong outcomes. There are a couple of things that I figure we ought to consider before beginning.

One of those is to decide whether we should exchange a countertrend framework or a drifting stock arrangement. It is possible that one can work, however it is dependent upon you to figure out which one you need to utilize. I suggest utilizing paper exchanging on a stock swing whenever you see one create.

This article will go top to bottom about a key swing exchanging system on every day outlines. While this might be viewed as cutting edge swing exchanging, this system is appropriate for all financial specialists. It is ideal for home investigation. We will disclose to you how to do appropriate specialized investigation and demonstrate to you when to enter the exchange and when to leave the exchange. We will do this by showing you how to set the correct benefit target.

It is imperative to ensure you have a completely created preparing plan before beginning to exchange any swing exchanging framework. This will enable you to plan to turn out to be increasingly effective and join the positions of expert informal investors. It is our objective to give you the exchanging openings, just as assistance you inside and out that we can to turn into the best swing brokers around. You can likewise get familiar with the manner in which financiers exchange the forex showcase.

The principle favorable position of swing exchanging is that it offers extraordinary hazard to reward exchanging openings. As such, you're going to hazard a littler measure of your record balance for a conceivably a lot greater benefit, contrasted with your hazard

The second advantage of utilizing swing exchanging procedures that work is that they will take out a great deal of the intraday commotion. Presently you'll be exchanging like the savvy cash does, which is in the huge swing waves.

The third advantage of swing exchanging depends on the utilization of specialized pointers. Utilizing specialized pointers can decrease the dangers of theoretical exchanging and help you to clarify choices. While some swing merchants focus on key markers too, they are not required for our straightforward systems.

The last advantage of utilizing a straightforward swing exchanging methodology is that you won't should be stuck to the screen for the entire day like with day exchanging procedures. A swing exchanging plan will work in all business sectors beginning from stocks, wares, Forex monetary standards and significantly more.

Like any exchanging technique, swing exchanging additionally has a couple of dangers. Since swing exchanging procedures take a few days or even a long time to play out, you face the dangers of "holes" in exchanging medium-term or throughout the end of the week.

Another danger of swing exchanging is that unexpected inversions can make losing positions. Since you are not exchanging all for the duration of the day, it very well may be anything but difficult to be found napping if value patterns don't happen as arranged. To diminish the danger of this occurrence, we prescribe giving stop orders with each new position. Stop requests can enable you "to secure" your increases and can likewise enable you to cut your misfortunes.

Moving Averages (MA)

Moving Averages put essentially are simply lines that are determined by past costs. They are straightforward and are very valuable with any exchanging sort, regardless of whether that is intraday, swing, or significantly longer exchanging styles.

You ought to consistently have various MA lines with separating timespans on your outline. I for one utilize three MAs: multi day MA, multi day MA, and a multi day MA. This gives me a more extensive perspective available and helps my recognize more grounded patterns and inversions.

Ways to Use Moving Averages: TRY IT

1.) Identifying Trend Strength

Put essentially, the more remote away the present cost and pattern are from its relative moving normal, the flimsier that pattern is, helping you the merchant, spot potential inversions and discovering passages and ways out. This strategy in great practice is utilized related to different markers like volume. (underneath).

2.) Identifying Trend Reversals with Crossovers

For the most part, MA hybrids can be signals for pattern inversions, for instance, if the nine-day MA crosses beneath the multi day MA after an upswing. At that point the bullish pattern might turn around flagging a bearish pattern. Be cautioned however, in light of the fact that there will in general be incessant phony outs with hybrids that find new dealers napping, you ought to consistently make a point to affirm inversions utilizing different techniques and devices.

Moving Averages are significant in light of the fact that they give brokers a comprehension of the business sectors state, never exchange indiscriminately.

Relative Strength Index (RSI)

The RSI pointer gives an overall assessment of the quality of a security's present value, utilizing it's past exhibition and instability. Once more, this is another must-have for a dealer as well as exchanging style.

The RSI scores a security on a size of 1–100, you should recollect this for the tips underneath.

RSI Can be Used a Number of Ways

1.) Identifying Overbought/Oversold Conditions

Recognizing overbought/oversold conditions is valuable in discovering pattern inversions or adjustments. At the point when a security is overbought it can flag a bearish pattern inversion or an adjustment, when a security is oversold it can flag a bullish pattern inversion or amendment.

The course book numbers for these conditions is 70/30: 70 = overbought/exaggerated, 30 oversold/underestimated. In spite of the fact that with an end goal to lessen phony outs, a few dealers (counting me) utilize 80/20 for those conditions.

2.) Identifying Divergences

Dealers can likewise utilize divergences to distinguish pattern inversions, a uniqueness is a distinction or difference (connection to Merriam Webster beneath).

Bullish Divergent Signal

At the point when the value makes a new low yet the RSI doesn't (or identical).

Bearish Divergent Signal

At the point when the value makes another high however the RSI doesn't (or proportional)

Brisk huge developments will make counterfeit outs (false flag). So simply like some other marker, consistently affirm patterns with different devices/techniques.

Volume

Utilizing Volume in exchanging is extremely straightforward, yet is typically ignored by new dealers. Clearly, it is significant for good liquidity however the standard that truly changed the manner in which I exchanged when I was learning was this.

"Patterns should be upheld by volume, consistently guarantee heavier volume is occurring toward a pattern."

Learning this improved my game significantly. At the point when an upturn in cost is in play, new cash should bolster it, so you have to see rising volume. The other way around with downtrends. If this isn't going on, at that point this is an indication of exaggerated or underestimated conditions.

The Basics Of Bollinger Bands

During the 1980s, John Bollinger, a long-term expert of the business sectors, built up the method of utilizing a moving normal with two exchanging groups above and underneath it. Dissimilar to a rate estimation from a typical moving normal, Bollinger Bands basically include and subtract a standard deviation count.

Standard deviation is a numerical equation that estimates instability, indicating how the stock cost can change from its actual worth. By estimating value instability, Bollinger Bands modify themselves to economic situations. This is the thing that makes them so convenient for brokers: they can discover practically the majority of the value information required between the two groups. Peruse on to discover how this marker functions, and how you can apply it to your exchanging.

What's a Bollinger Band?

Bollinger Bands comprise of an inside line and two value channels (groups) above and underneath it. The inside line is an exponential moving normal; the value channels are the standard deviations of the stock being considered. The groups will grow and contract as the value activity of an issue ends up unstable (development) or ends up bound into a tight exchanging example (compression).

A stock may exchange for significant stretches in a pattern, but with some unpredictability every once in a while. To all the more likely observe the pattern, brokers utilize the moving normal to channel the value activity. Along these lines, brokers can assemble significant data about how the market is exchanging. For instance, after a sharp ascent or fall in the pattern, the market may merge, exchanging a thin design and bungling above and underneath the moving normal. To all the more likely screen this conduct, merchants utilize the value channels, which incorporate the exchanging action around the pattern.

We realize that business sectors exchange unpredictably regularly despite the fact that they are as yet exchanging an upswing or downtrend. Professionals utilize moving midpoints with help and opposition lines to envision the value activity of a stock. Upper obstruction and lower bolster lines are first attracted and after that extrapolated to frame channels inside which the merchant anticipates that costs should be contained. A few brokers draw straight lines associating either tops or bottoms of costs to distinguish the upper or lower value limits, separately, and afterward add parallel lines to characterize the channel inside which the costs should move. For whatever length of time that costs don't move out of this channel, the broker can be sensibly certain that costs are moving true to form.

At the point when stock costs constantly contact the upper Bollinger Band®, the costs are believed to be overbought; on the other hand, when they persistently contact the lower band, costs are believed to be oversold, setting off a purchase signal.

When utilizing Bollinger Bands, assign the upper and lower groups as value targets. If the value avoids off the lower band and crosses over the 20-day normal (the center line), the upper band comes to speak to the upper value target. In a solid upturn, costs normally vary between the upper band and the 20-day moving normal. At the point when that occurs, a crossin